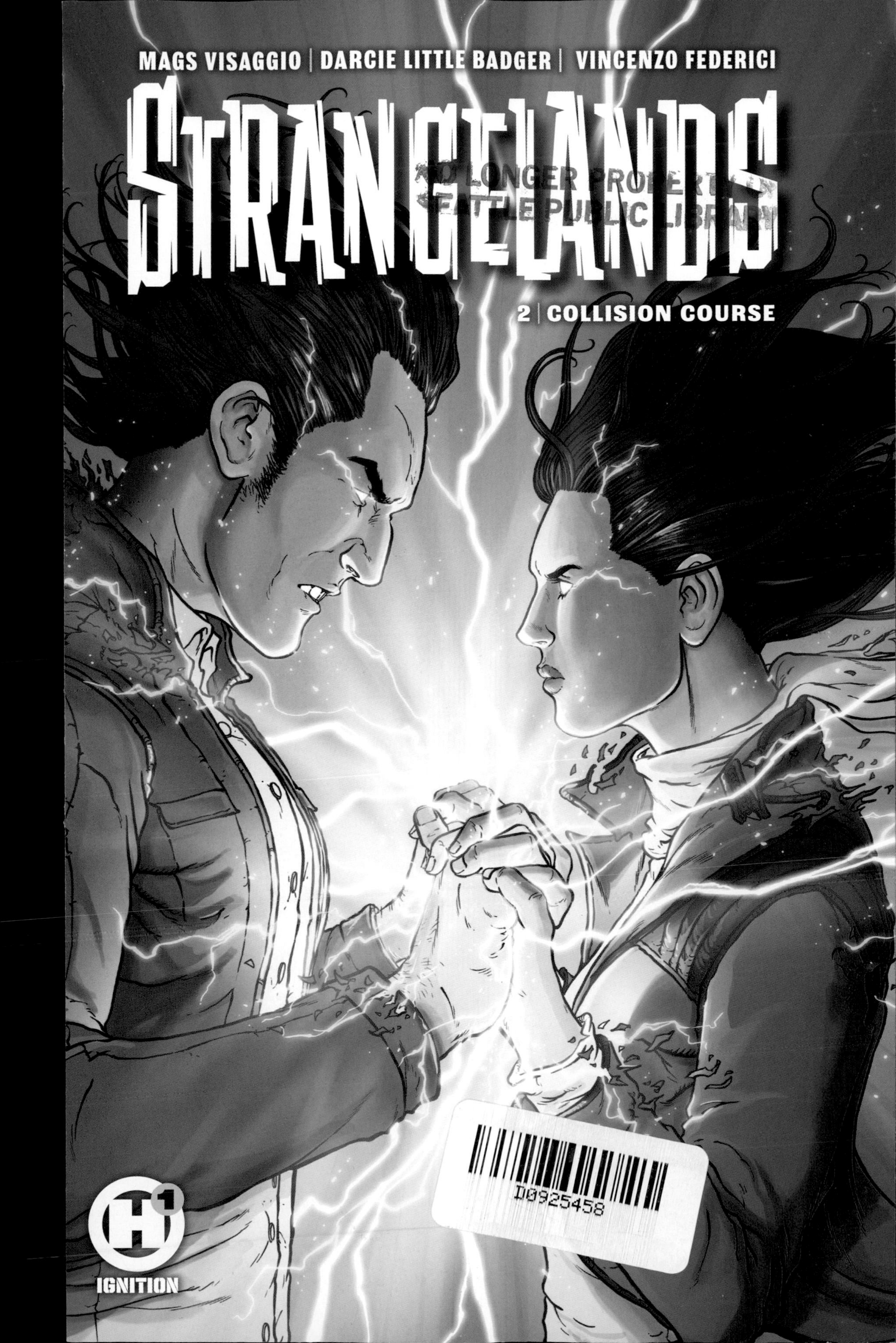
MAGS VISAGGIO | DARCIE LITTLE BADGER | VINCENZO FEDERICI
STRANGELANDS
2 | COLLISION COURSE
H1
IGNITION

WRITERS | **MAGS VISAGGIO** AND
DARCIE LITTLE BADGER
ARTIST | **VINCENZO FEDERICI**
COLOR ARTIST | **REX LOKUS**
COVER | **JOHN CASSADAY & LAURA MARTIN**
TITLE PAGE ILLUSTRATION | **JON DAVIS-HUNT**
LETTERS | **A LARGER WORLD STUDIOS**

SHARED UNIVERSE BASED ON CONCEPTS CREATED WITH
KWANZA OSAJYEFO, CARLA SPEED MCNEIL, YANICK PAQUETTE

PUBLISHER | **MARK WAID**
CHIEF CREATIVE OFFICER | **JOHN CASSADAY**
SENIOR EDITOR | **ROB LEVIN**
ASSISTANT EDITOR | **AMANDA LUCIDO**
LOGO DESIGN | **RIAN HUGHES**
SENIOR ART DIRECTOR | **JERRY FRISSEN**
JUNIOR DESIGNER | **RYAN LEWIS**

CEO | **FABRICE GIGER**
COO | **ALEX DONOGHUE**
CFO | **GUILLAUME NOUGARET**
SALES MANAGER | **PEDRO HERNANDEZ**
MARKETING ASSISTANT | **ANDREA TORRES**
SALES REPRESENTATIVE | **HARLEY SALBACKA**
PRODUCTION COORDINATOR | **ALISA TRAGER**
DIRECTOR, LICENSING | **EDMOND LEE**
CTO | **BRUNO BARBERI**
RIGHTS AND LICENSING | **LICENSING@HUMANOIDS.COM**
PRESS AND SOCIAL MEDIA | **PR@HUMANOIDS.COM**

STRANGELANDS, VOL. 2 This title is a publication of Humanoids, Inc. 8033 Sunset Blvd. #628, Los Angeles, CA 90046. Copyright © 2020 Humanoids, Inc., Los Angeles (USA). All rights reserved. Humanoids and its logos are ® and © 2020 Humanoids, Inc.
Library of Congress Control Number: 2019910049

This volume collects STRANGELANDS issues 5-8.

H1 is an imprint of Humanoids, Inc.

HUMANOIDS

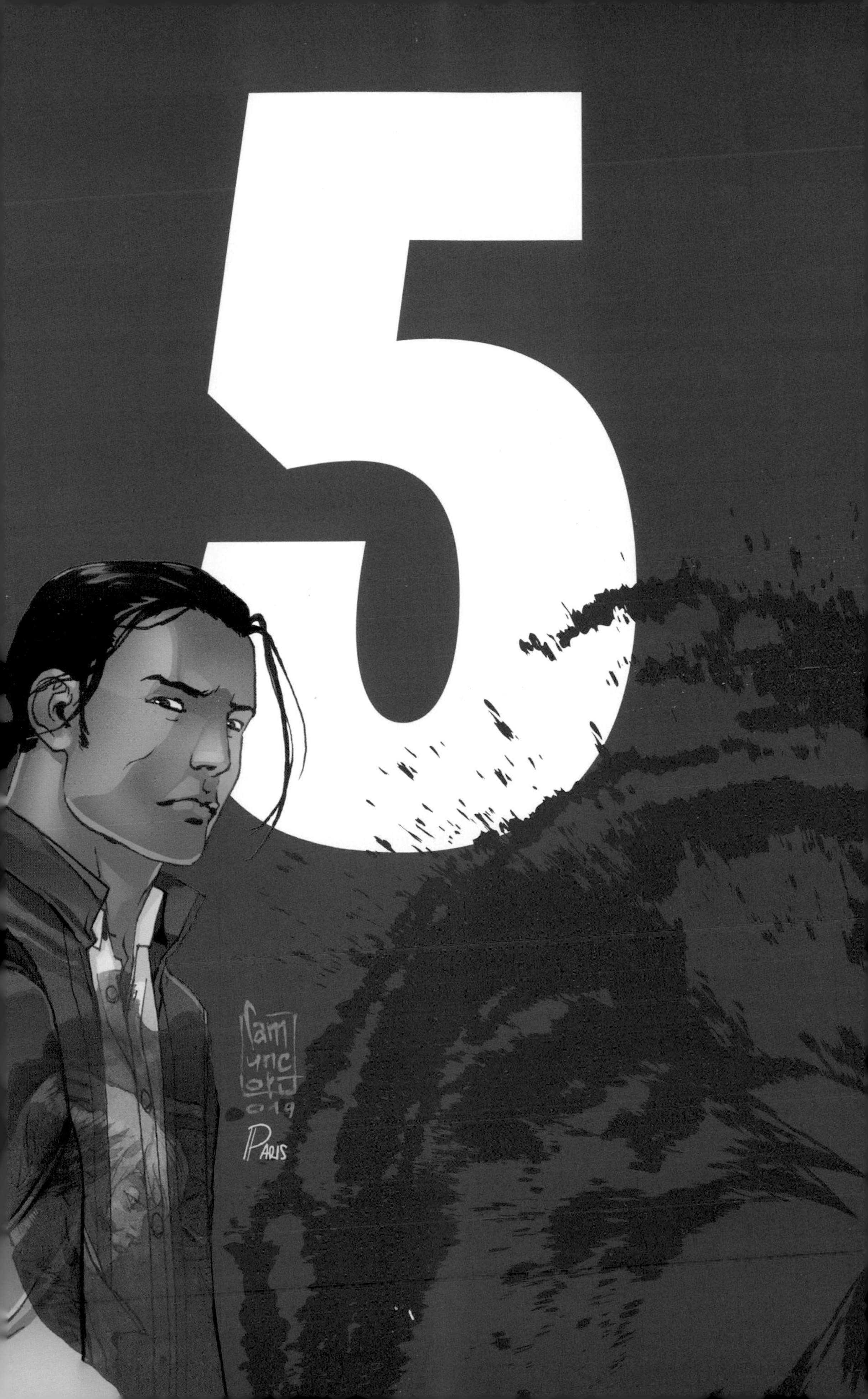
5
PARIS

OUR WORLD'S DNA IS CHANGING.

UNPRECEDENTED TECTONIC SHIFTS.
SPONTANEOUS, RADICAL CHANGES IN THE ECO SYSTEMS.

IN MOMENTS OF UNIMAGINABLE AGITATION,
THE HUMAN RACE ACTS OUT IN UNIMAGINABLE WAYS.

AND THOSE ARE JUST INDIVIDUAL SPECIES. NOW EARTH ITSELF IS PUSHING BACK.

CERTAIN PEOPLE WORLDWIDE ARE ... CHANGING. ***TRANSFORMING***.

IGNITING WITH ***POWER***.

H1 IGNITION

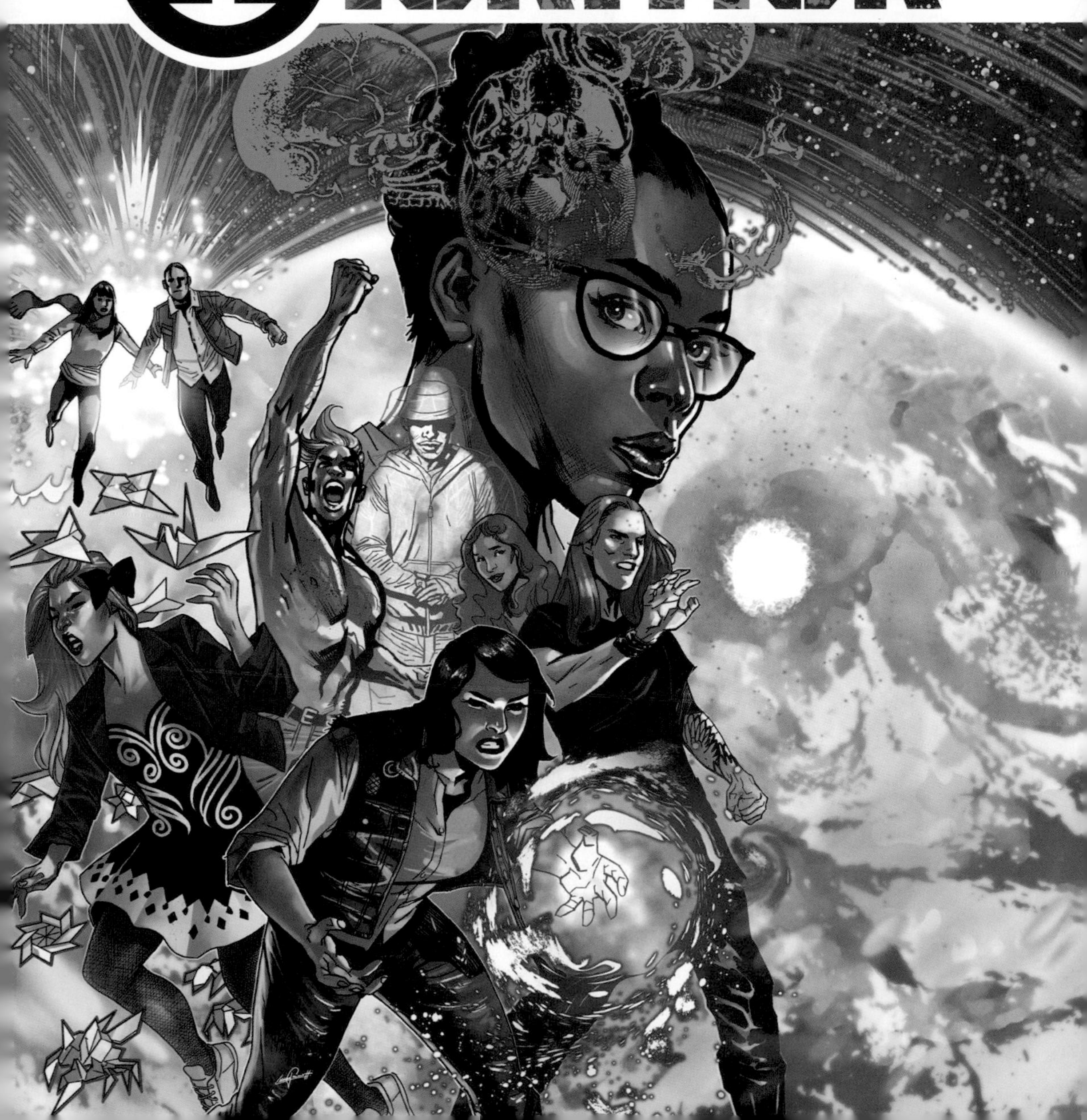

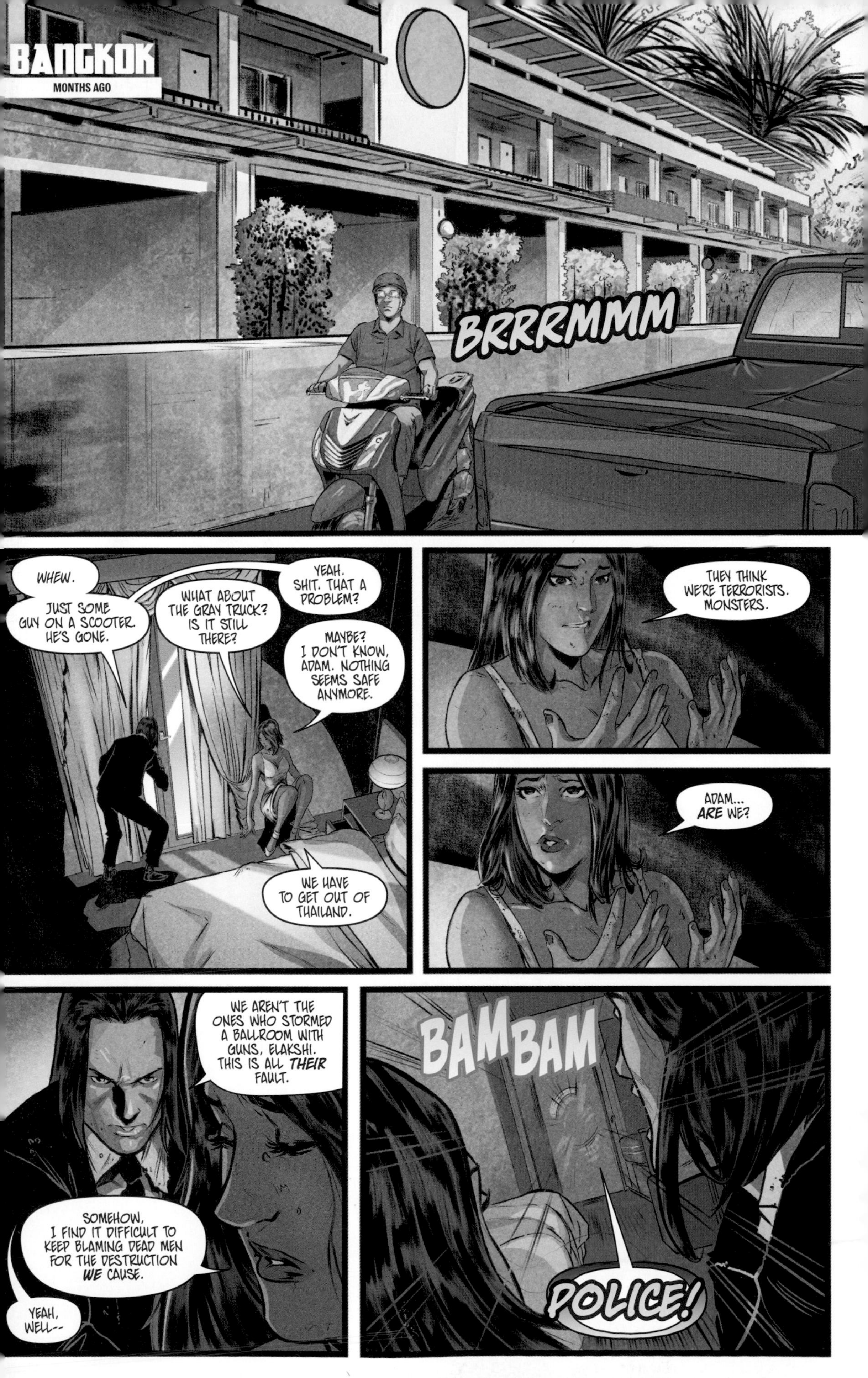
BANGKOK
MONTHS AGO
BRRRMMM
WHEW.
JUST SOME GUY ON A SCOOTER. HE'S GONE.
WHAT ABOUT THE GRAY TRUCK? IS IT STILL THERE?
YEAH. SHIT. THAT A PROBLEM?
MAYBE? I DON'T KNOW, ADAM. NOTHING SEEMS SAFE ANYMORE.
WE HAVE TO GET OUT OF THAILAND.
THEY THINK WE'RE TERRORISTS. MONSTERS.
ADAM... ARE WE?
WE AREN'T THE ONES WHO STORMED A BALLROOM WITH GUNS, ELAKSHI. THIS IS ALL THEIR FAULT.
SOMEHOW, I FIND IT DIFFICULT TO KEEP BLAMING DEAD MEN FOR THE DESTRUCTION WE CAUSE.
YEAH, WELL--
BAM BAM
POLICE!

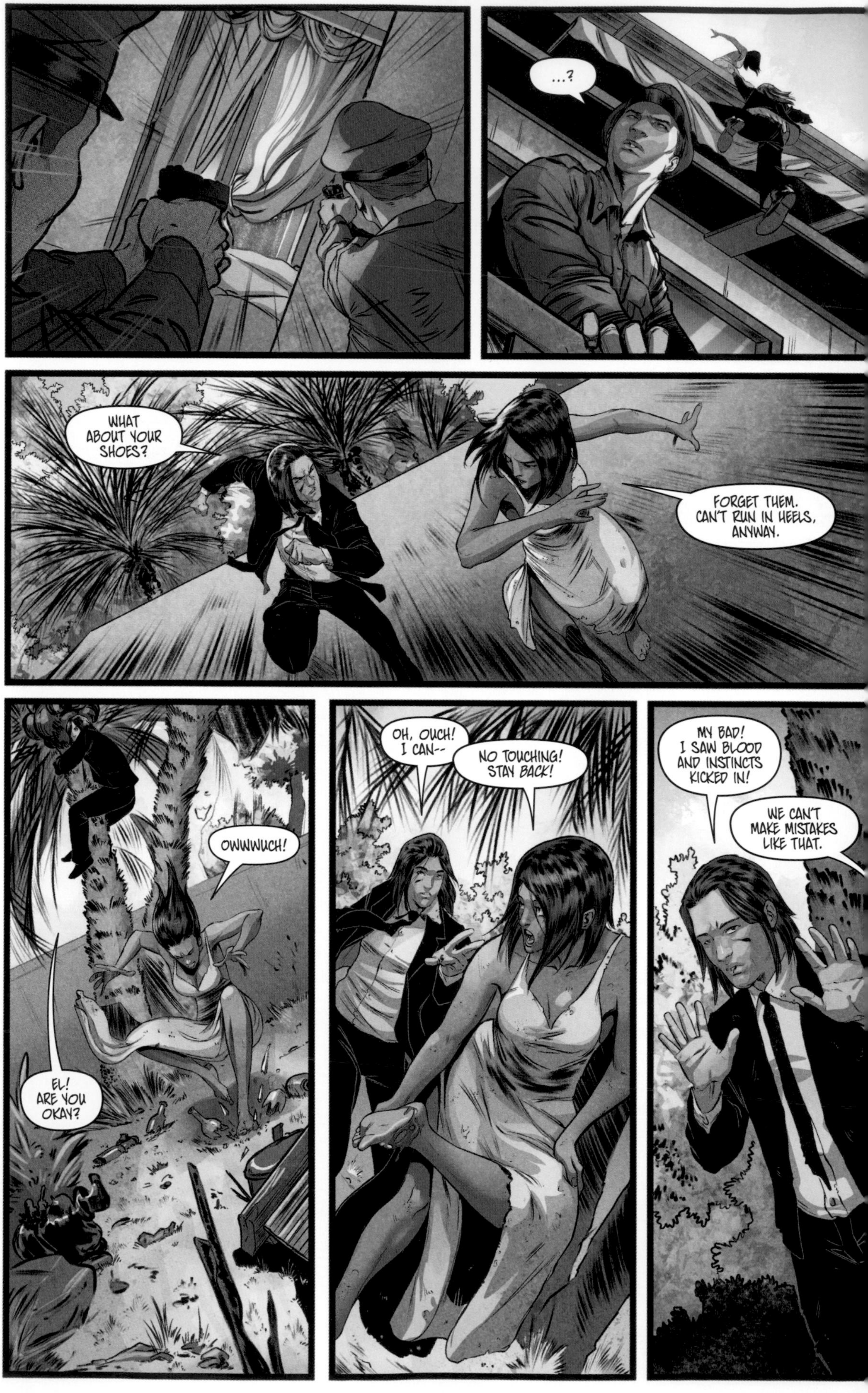
...?
WHAT ABOUT YOUR SHOES?
FORGET THEM. CAN'T RUN IN HEELS, ANYWAY.
OWWWUCH!
EL! ARE YOU OKAY?
OH, OUCH! I CAN--
NO TOUCHING! STAY BACK!
MY BAD! I SAW BLOOD AND INSTINCTS KICKED IN!
WE CAN'T MAKE MISTAKES LIKE THAT.

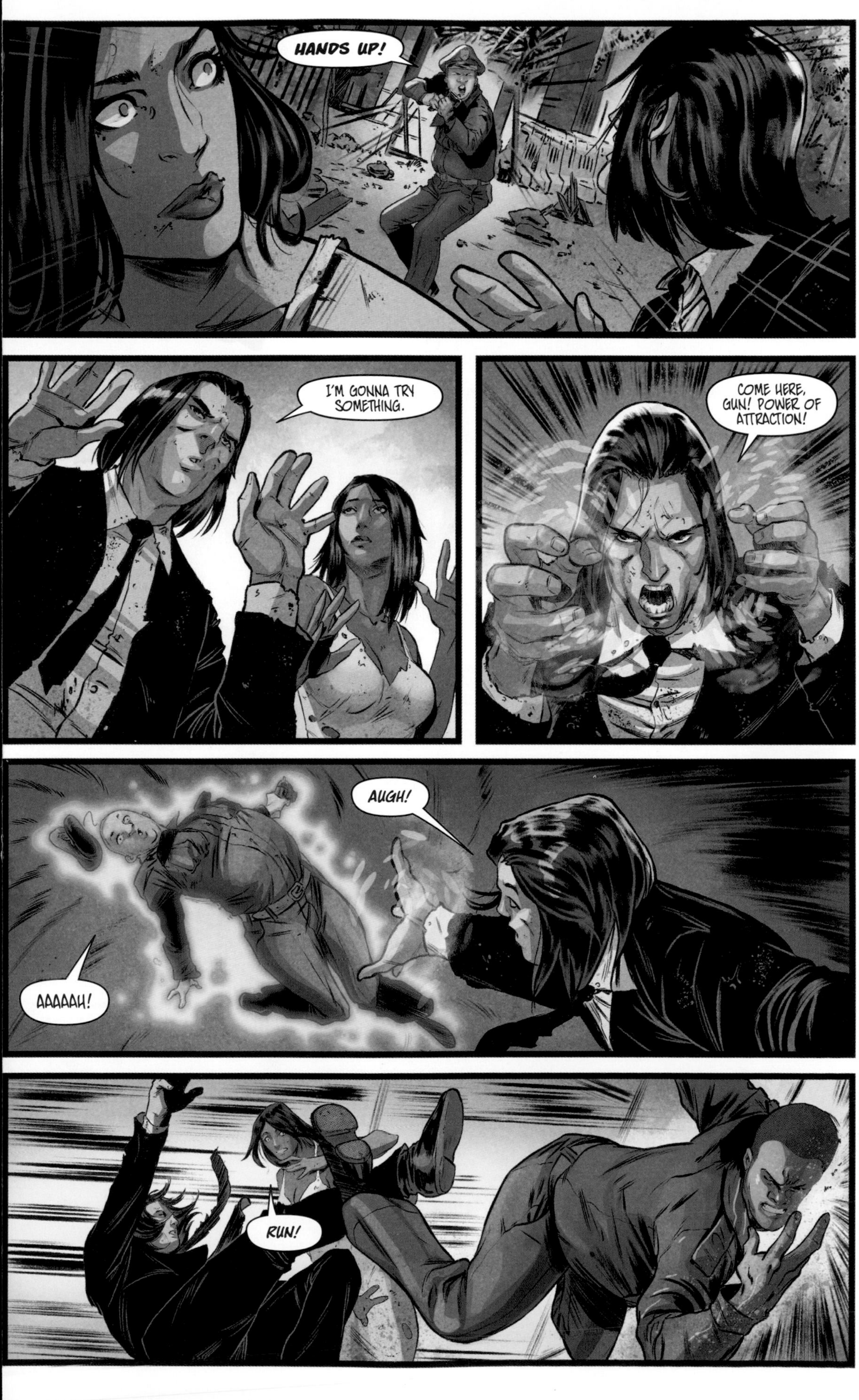
HANDS UP!
I'M GONNA TRY SOMETHING.
COME HERE, GUN! POWER OF ATTRACTION!
AUGH!
AAAAAH!
RUN!

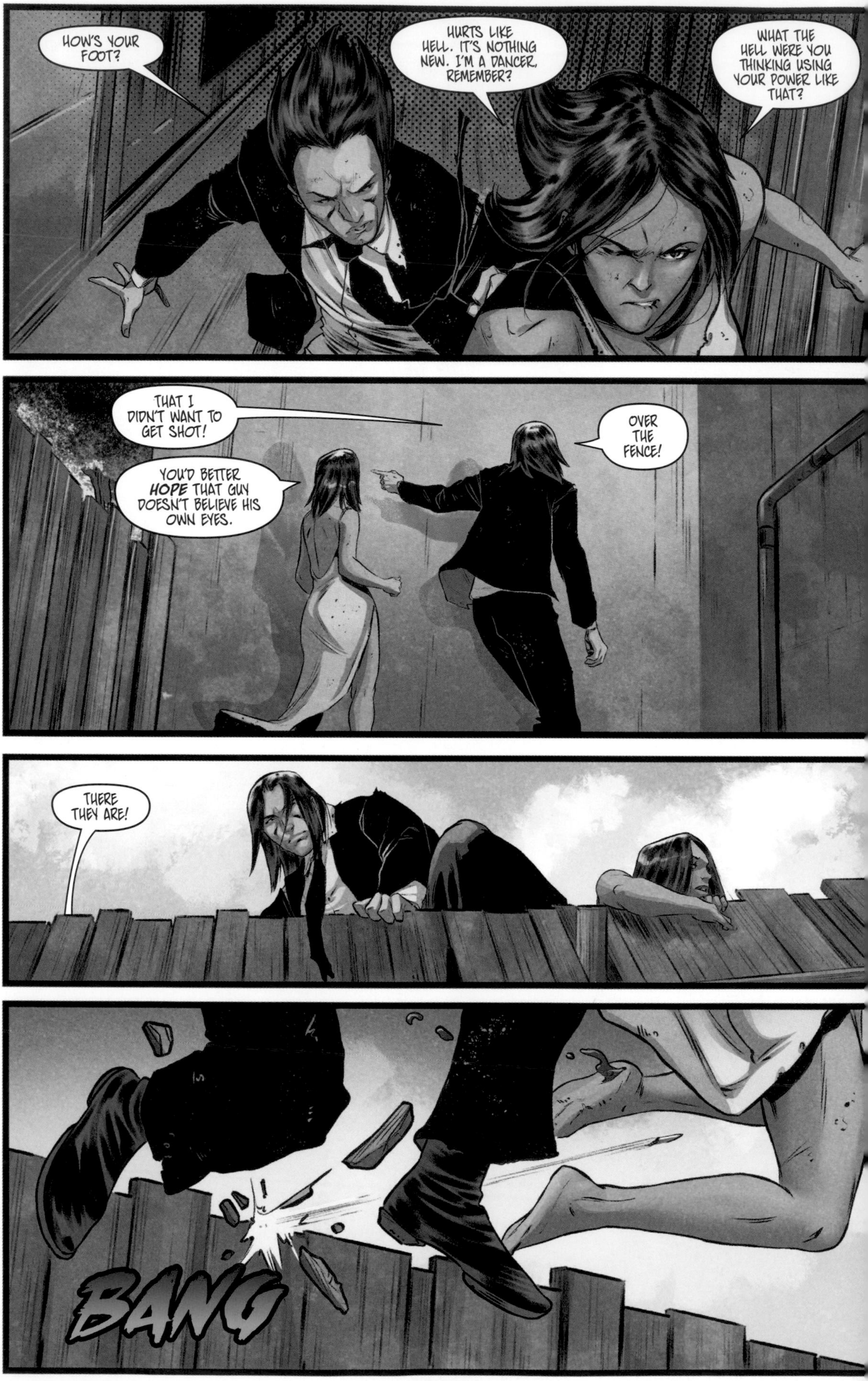
HOW'S YOUR FOOT?
HURTS LIKE HELL. IT'S NOTHING NEW. I'M A DANCER, REMEMBER?
WHAT THE HELL WERE YOU THINKING USING YOUR POWER LIKE THAT?
THAT I DIDN'T WANT TO GET SHOT!
YOU'D BETTER HOPE THAT GUY DOESN'T BELIEVE HIS OWN EYES.
OVER THE FENCE!
THERE THEY ARE!
BANG

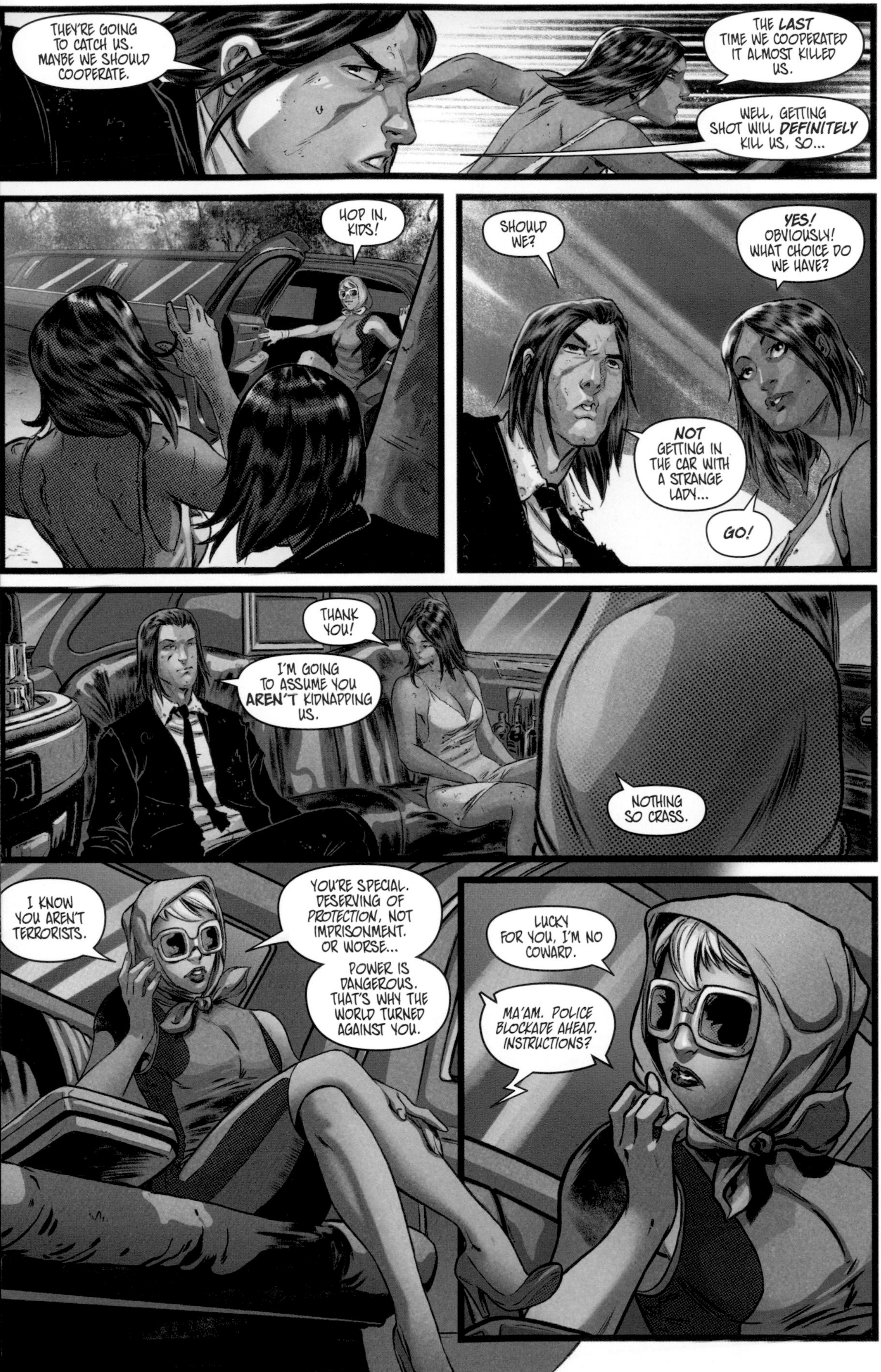
THEY'RE GOING TO CATCH US. MAYBE WE SHOULD COOPERATE.
THE **LAST** TIME WE COOPERATED IT ALMOST KILLED US.
WELL, GETTING SHOT WILL **DEFINITELY** KILL US, SO...
HOP IN, KIDS!
SHOULD WE?
YES! OBVIOUSLY! WHAT CHOICE DO WE HAVE?
NOT GETTING IN THE CAR WITH A STRANGE LADY...
GO!
THANK YOU!
I'M GOING TO ASSUME YOU **AREN'T** KIDNAPPING US.
NOTHING SO CRASS.
I KNOW YOU AREN'T TERRORISTS.
YOU'RE SPECIAL. DESERVING OF PROTECTION, NOT IMPRISONMENT. OR WORSE...
POWER IS DANGEROUS. THAT'S WHY THE WORLD TURNED AGAINST YOU.
LUCKY FOR YOU, I'M NO COWARD.
MA'AM. POLICE BLOCKADE AHEAD. INSTRUCTIONS?

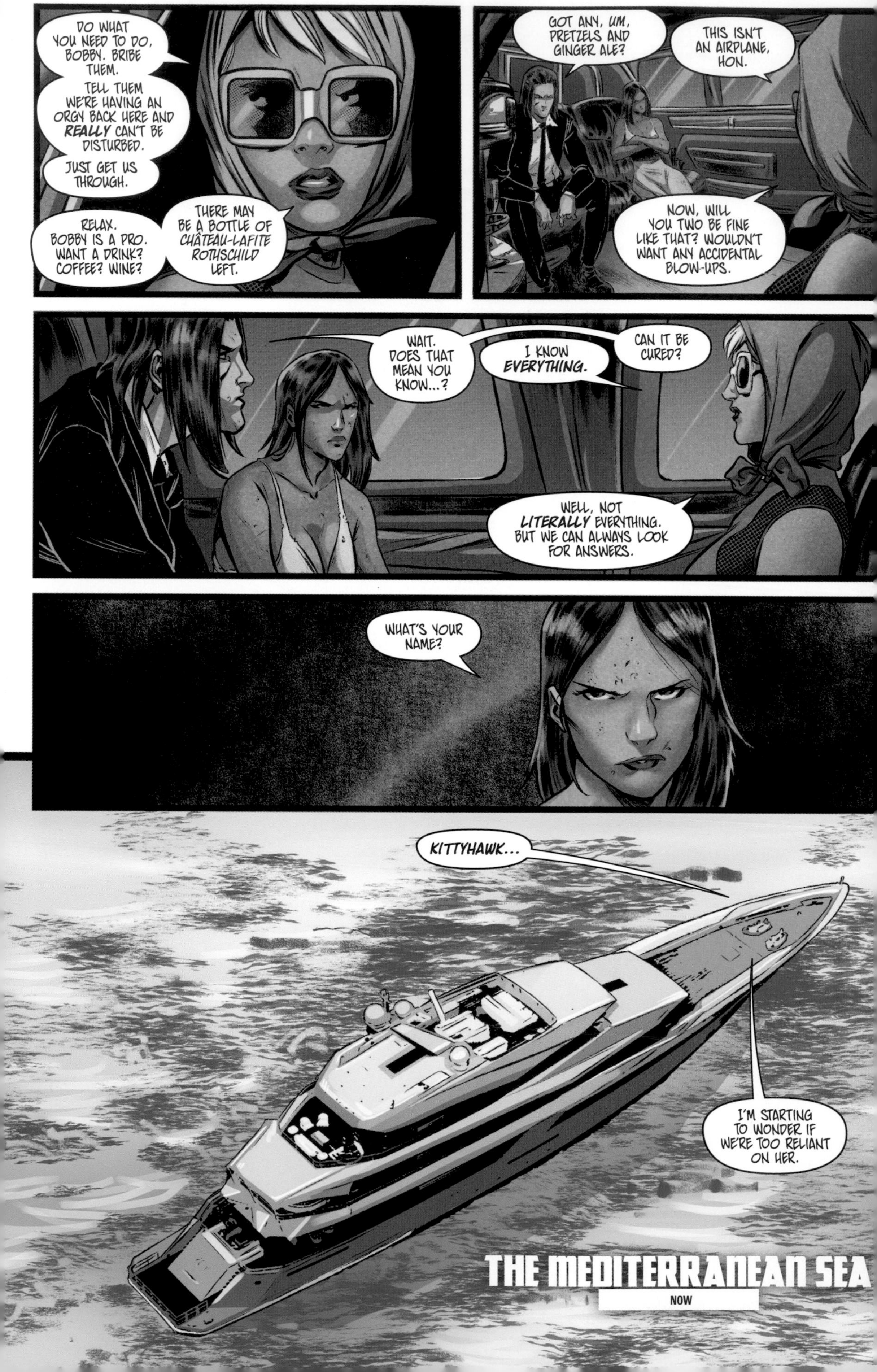
DO WHAT YOU NEED TO DO, BOBBY. BRIBE THEM.
TELL THEM WE'RE HAVING AN ORGY BACK HERE AND REALLY CAN'T BE DISTURBED.
JUST GET US THROUGH.
RELAX. BOBBY IS A PRO. WANT A DRINK? COFFEE? WINE?
THERE MAY BE A BOTTLE OF CHÂTEAU-LAFITE ROTHSCHILD LEFT.
GOT ANY, UM, PRETZELS AND GINGER ALE?
THIS ISN'T AN AIRPLANE, HON.
NOW, WILL YOU TWO BE FINE LIKE THAT? WOULDN'T WANT ANY ACCIDENTAL BLOW-UPS.
WAIT. DOES THAT MEAN YOU KNOW...?
CAN IT BE CURED?
I KNOW EVERYTHING.
WELL, NOT LITERALLY EVERYTHING. BUT WE CAN ALWAYS LOOK FOR ANSWERS.
WHAT'S YOUR NAME?
KITTYHAWK...
I'M STARTING TO WONDER IF WE'RE TOO RELIANT ON HER.
THE MEDITERRANEAN SEA
NOW

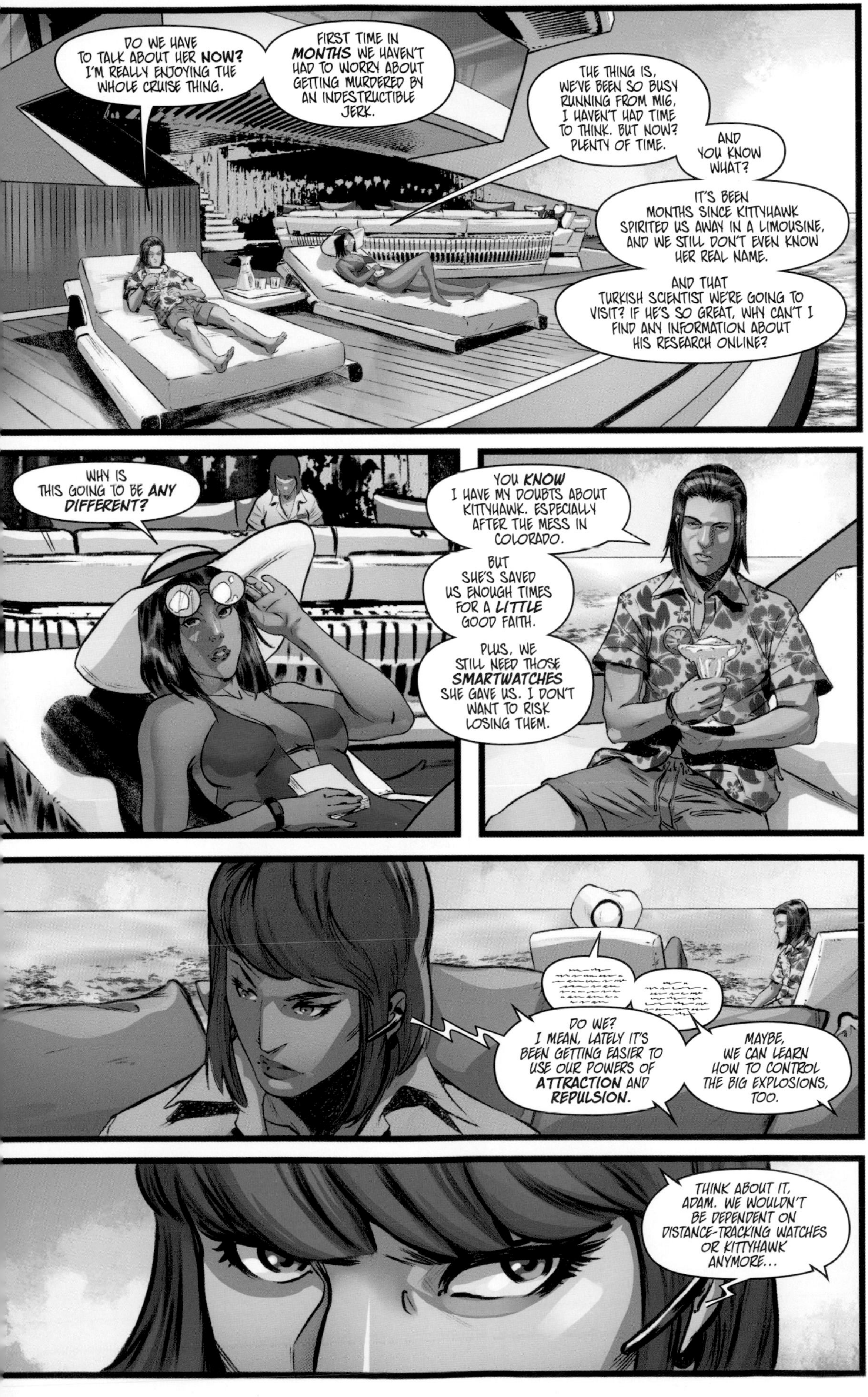
DO WE HAVE TO TALK ABOUT HER NOW? I'M REALLY ENJOYING THE WHOLE CRUISE THING.
FIRST TIME IN MONTHS WE HAVEN'T HAD TO WORRY ABOUT GETTING MURDERED BY AN INDESTRUCTIBLE JERK.
THE THING IS, WE'VE BEEN SO BUSY RUNNING FROM MI6, I HAVEN'T HAD TIME TO THINK. BUT NOW? PLENTY OF TIME.
AND YOU KNOW WHAT?
IT'S BEEN MONTHS SINCE KITTYHAWK SPIRITED US AWAY IN A LIMOUSINE, AND WE STILL DON'T EVEN KNOW HER REAL NAME.
AND THAT TURKISH SCIENTIST WE'RE GOING TO VISIT? IF HE'S SO GREAT, WHY CAN'T I FIND ANY INFORMATION ABOUT HIS RESEARCH ONLINE?
WHY IS THIS GOING TO BE ANY DIFFERENT?
YOU KNOW I HAVE MY DOUBTS ABOUT KITTYHAWK. ESPECIALLY AFTER THE MESS IN COLORADO.
BUT SHE'S SAVED US ENOUGH TIMES FOR A LITTLE GOOD FAITH.
PLUS, WE STILL NEED THOSE SMARTWATCHES SHE GAVE US. I DON'T WANT TO RISK LOSING THEM.
DO WE? I MEAN, LATELY IT'S BEEN GETTING EASIER TO USE OUR POWERS OF ATTRACTION AND REPULSION.
MAYBE, WE CAN LEARN HOW TO CONTROL THE BIG EXPLOSIONS, TOO.
THINK ABOUT IT, ADAM. WE WOULDN'T BE DEPENDENT ON DISTANCE-TRACKING WATCHES OR KITTYHAWK ANYMORE...

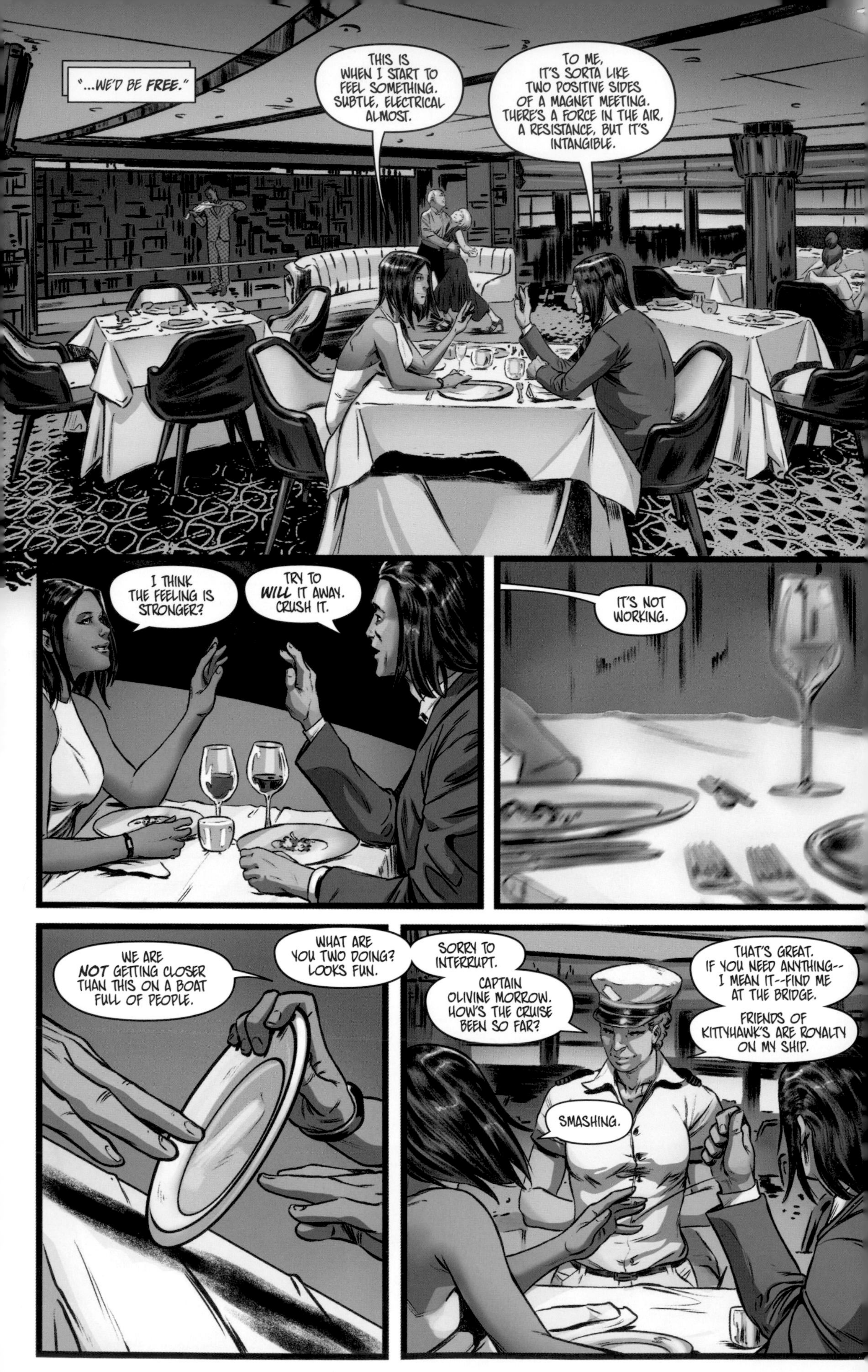
"...WE'D BE FREE."
THIS IS WHEN I START TO FEEL SOMETHING. SUBTLE, ELECTRICAL ALMOST.
TO ME, IT'S SORTA LIKE TWO POSITIVE SIDES OF A MAGNET MEETING. THERE'S A FORCE IN THE AIR, A RESISTANCE, BUT IT'S INTANGIBLE.
I THINK THE FEELING IS STRONGER?
TRY TO WILL IT AWAY. CRUSH IT.
IT'S NOT WORKING.
WE ARE NOT GETTING CLOSER THAN THIS ON A BOAT FULL OF PEOPLE.
WHAT ARE YOU TWO DOING? LOOKS FUN.
SORRY TO INTERRUPT.
CAPTAIN OLIVINE MORROW. HOW'S THE CRUISE BEEN SO FAR?
SMASHING.
THAT'S GREAT. IF YOU NEED ANYTHING-- I MEAN IT--FIND ME AT THE BRIDGE.
FRIENDS OF KITTYHAWK'S ARE ROYALTY ON MY SHIP.

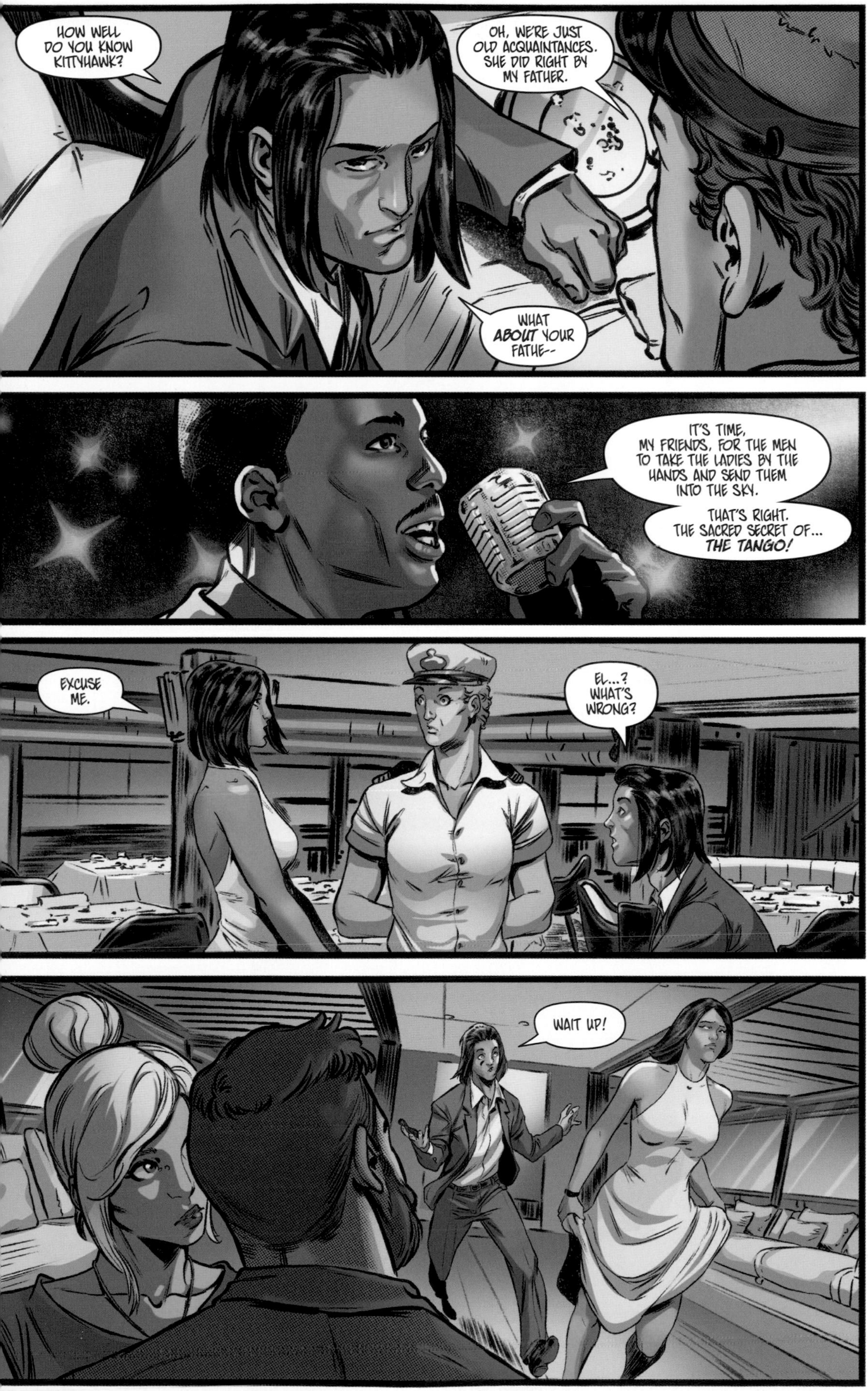
HOW WELL DO YOU KNOW KITTYHAWK?
OH, WE'RE JUST OLD ACQUAINTANCES. SHE DID RIGHT BY MY FATHER.
WHAT ABOUT YOUR FATHE--
IT'S TIME, MY FRIENDS, FOR THE MEN TO TAKE THE LADIES BY THE HANDS AND SEND THEM INTO THE SKY.
THAT'S RIGHT. THE SACRED SECRET OF... THE TANGO!
EXCUSE ME.
EL...? WHAT'S WRONG?
WAIT UP!

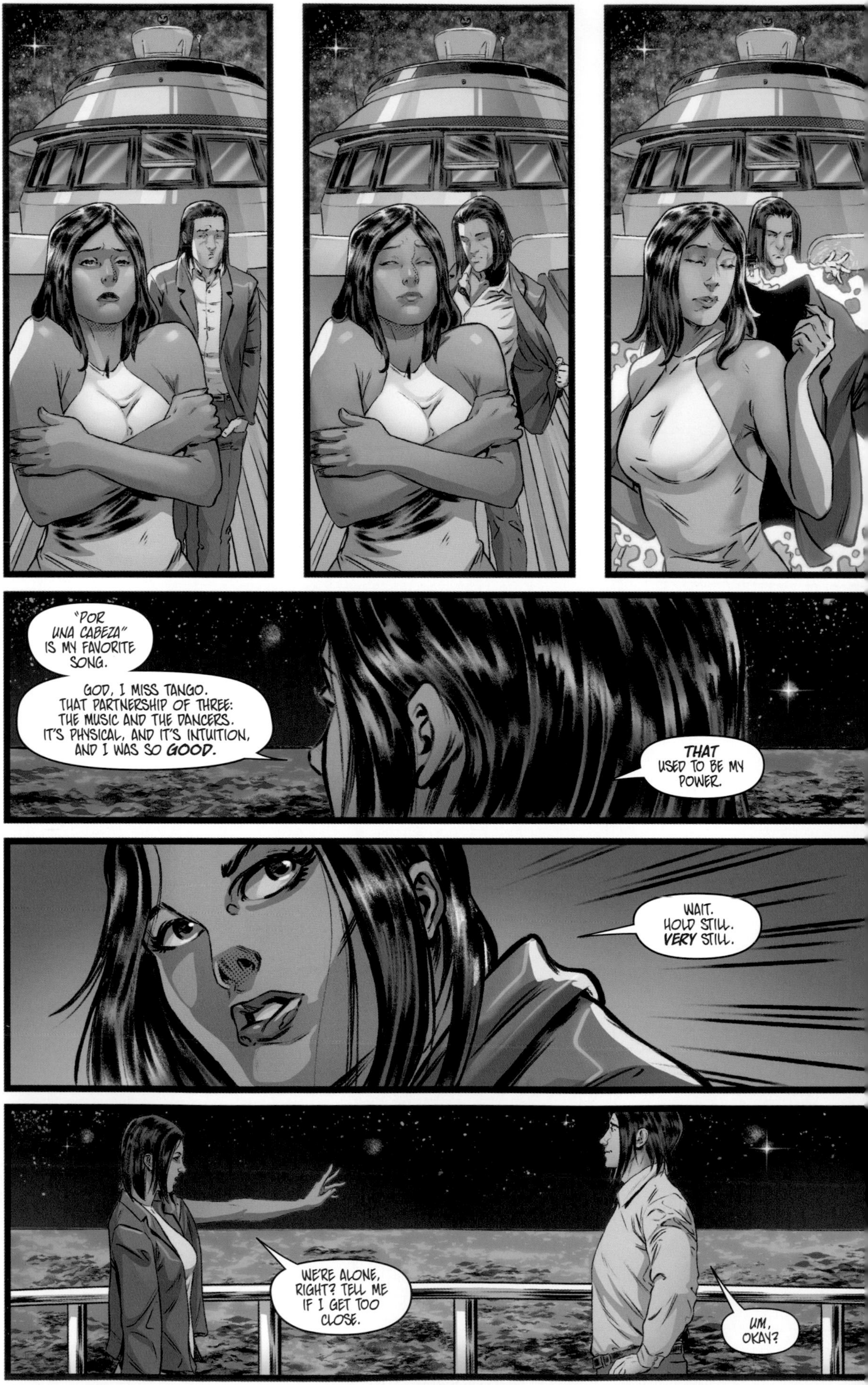
"POR UNA CABEZA" IS MY FAVORITE SONG.
GOD, I MISS TANGO. THAT PARTNERSHIP OF THREE: THE MUSIC AND THE DANCERS. IT'S PHYSICAL, AND IT'S INTUITION, AND I WAS SO GOOD.
THAT USED TO BE MY POWER.
WAIT. HOLD STILL. VERY STILL.
WE'RE ALONE, RIGHT? TELL ME IF I GET TOO CLOSE.
UM, OKAY?

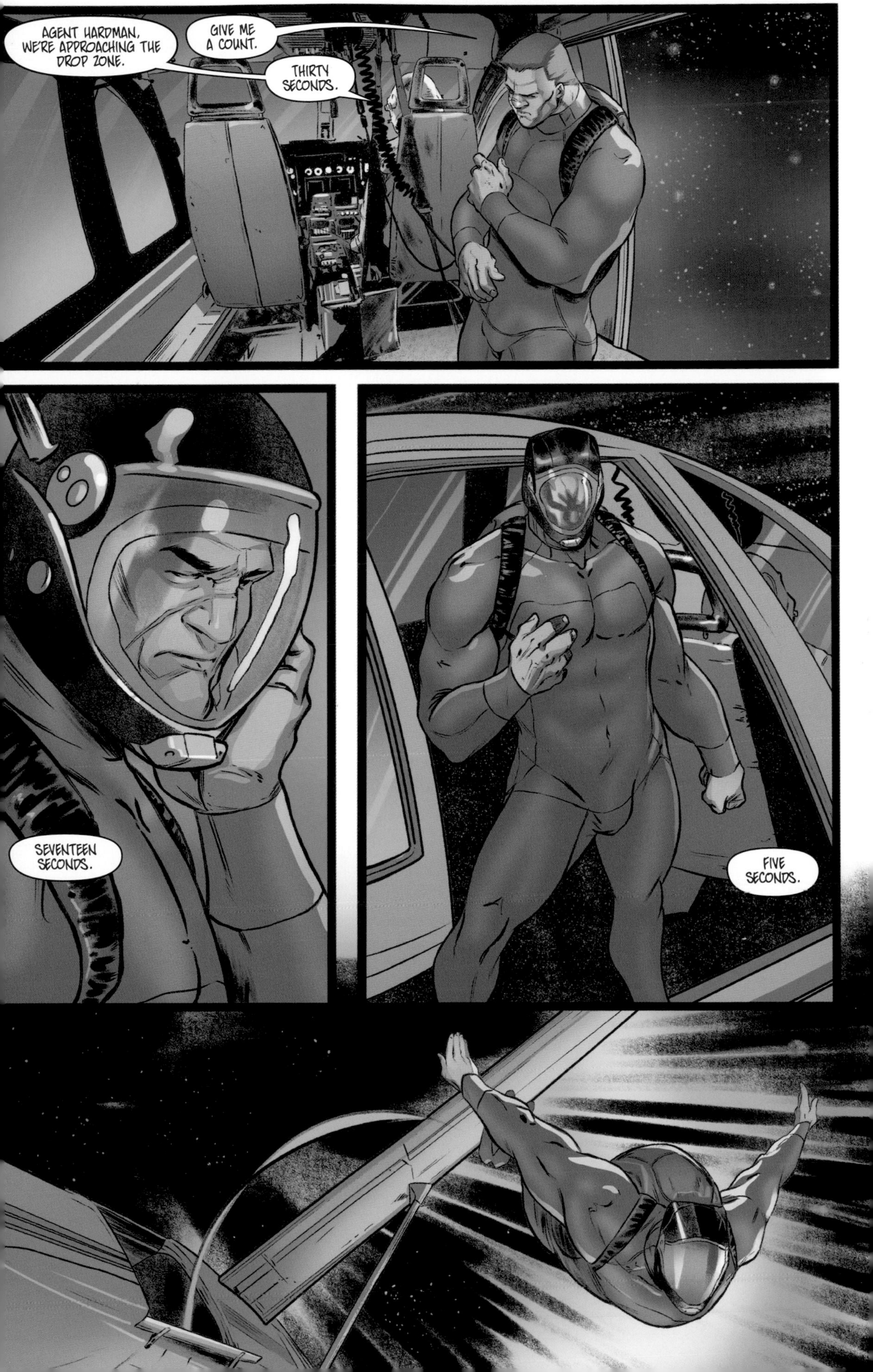
AGENT HARDMAN, WE'RE APPROACHING THE DROP ZONE.
GIVE ME A COUNT.
THIRTY SECONDS.
SEVENTEEN SECONDS.
FIVE SECONDS.

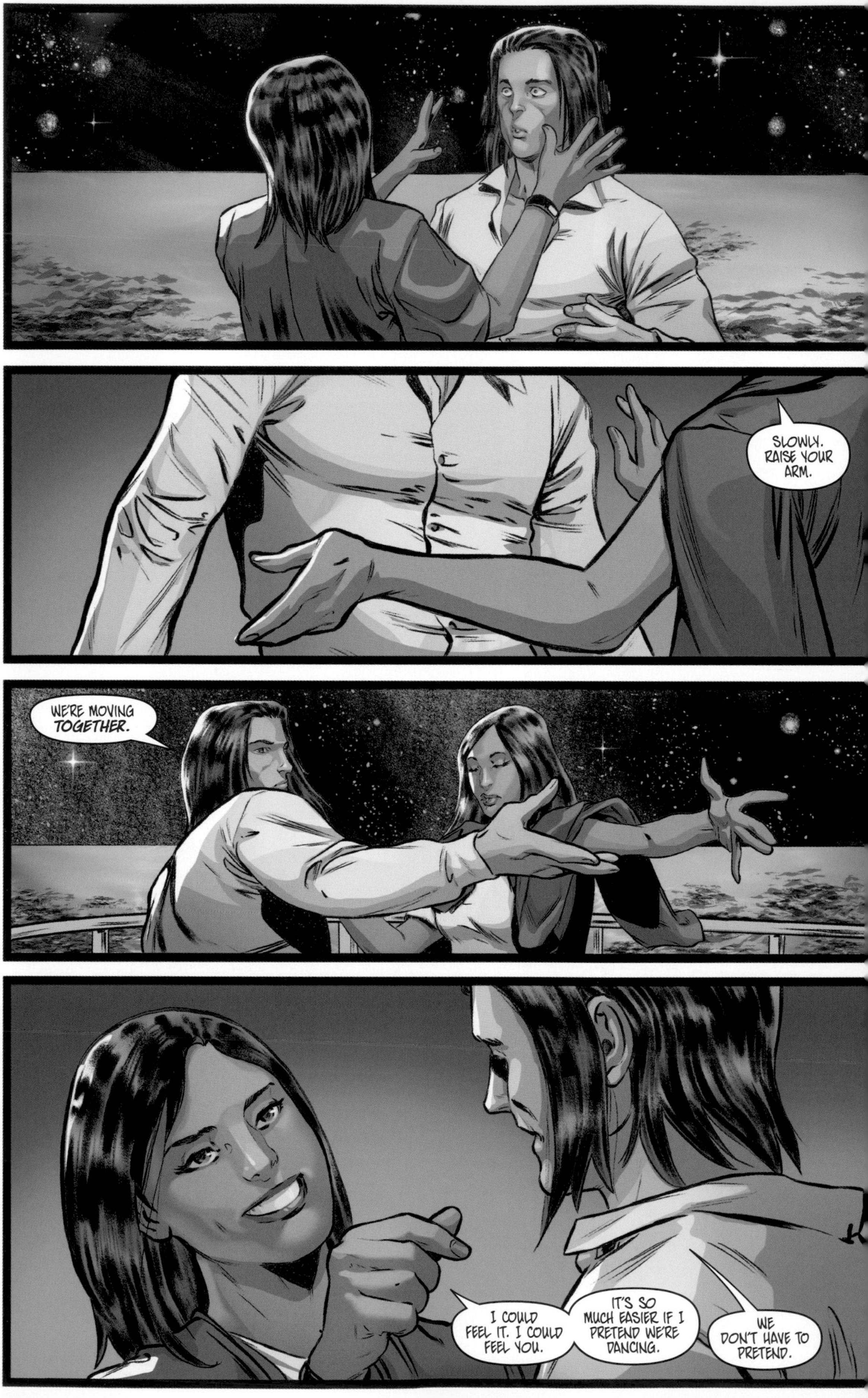
SLOWLY. RAISE YOUR ARM.
WE'RE MOVING TOGETHER.
I COULD FEEL IT. I COULD FEEL YOU.
IT'S SO MUCH EASIER IF I PRETEND WE'RE DANCING.
WE DON'T HAVE TO PRETEND.

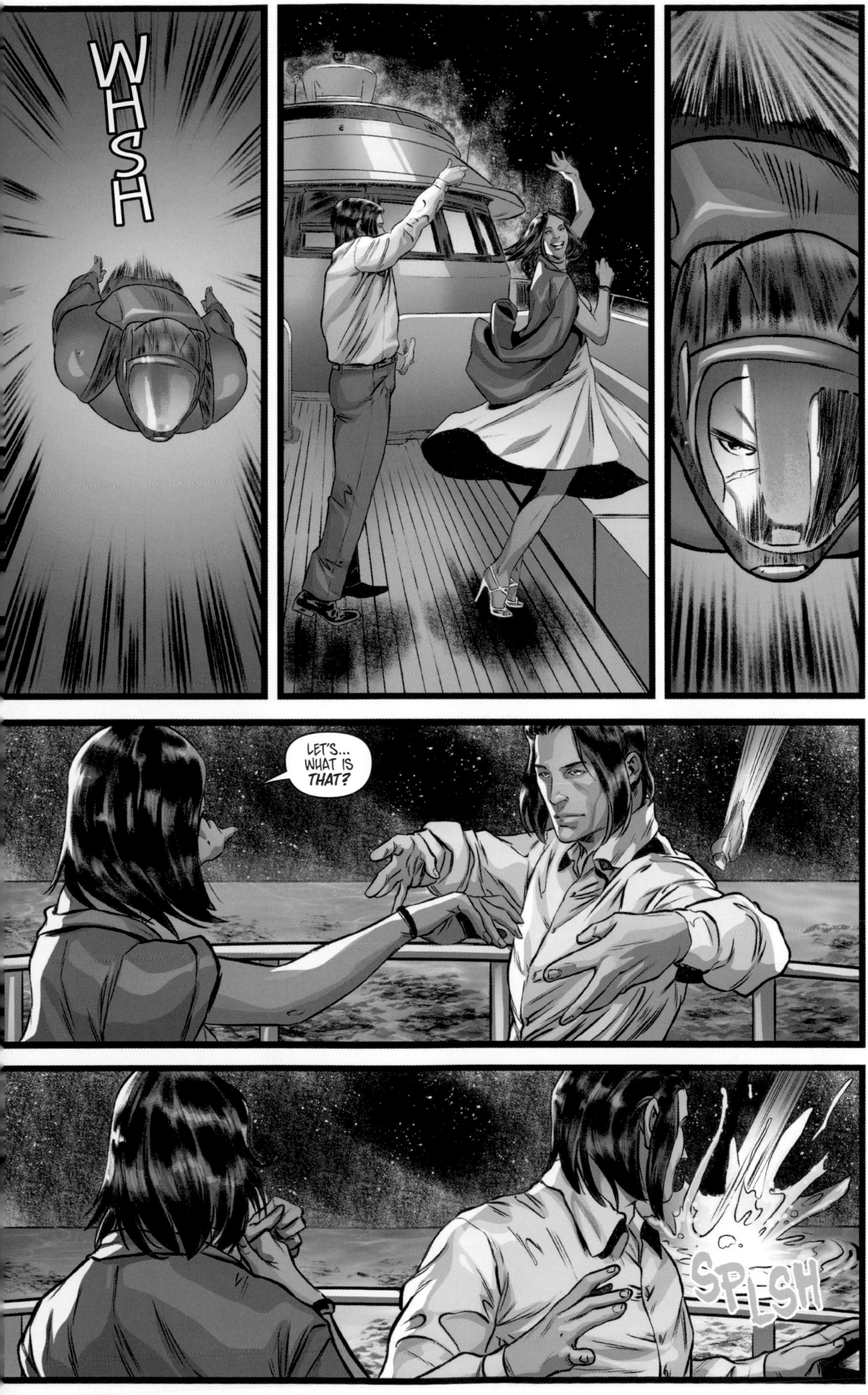
WHSH
LET'S... WHAT IS THAT?
SPLSH

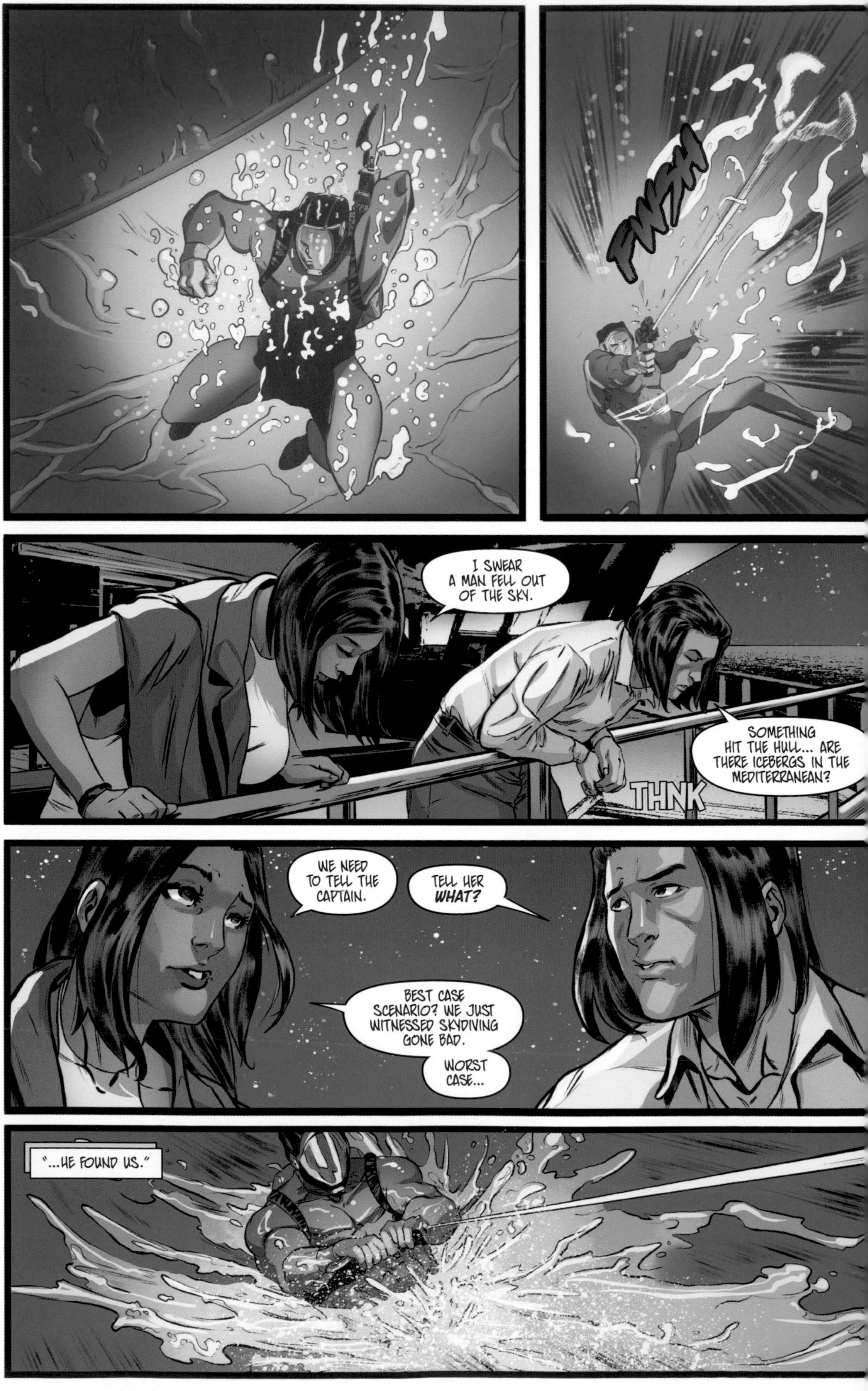
FWSH
I SWEAR A MAN FELL OUT OF THE SKY.
SOMETHING HIT THE HULL... ARE THERE ICEBERGS IN THE MEDITERRANEAN?
THNK
WE NEED TO TELL THE CAPTAIN.
TELL HER *WHAT?*
BEST CASE SCENARIO? WE JUST WITNESSED SKYDIVING GONE BAD.
WORST CASE...
"...HE FOUND US."

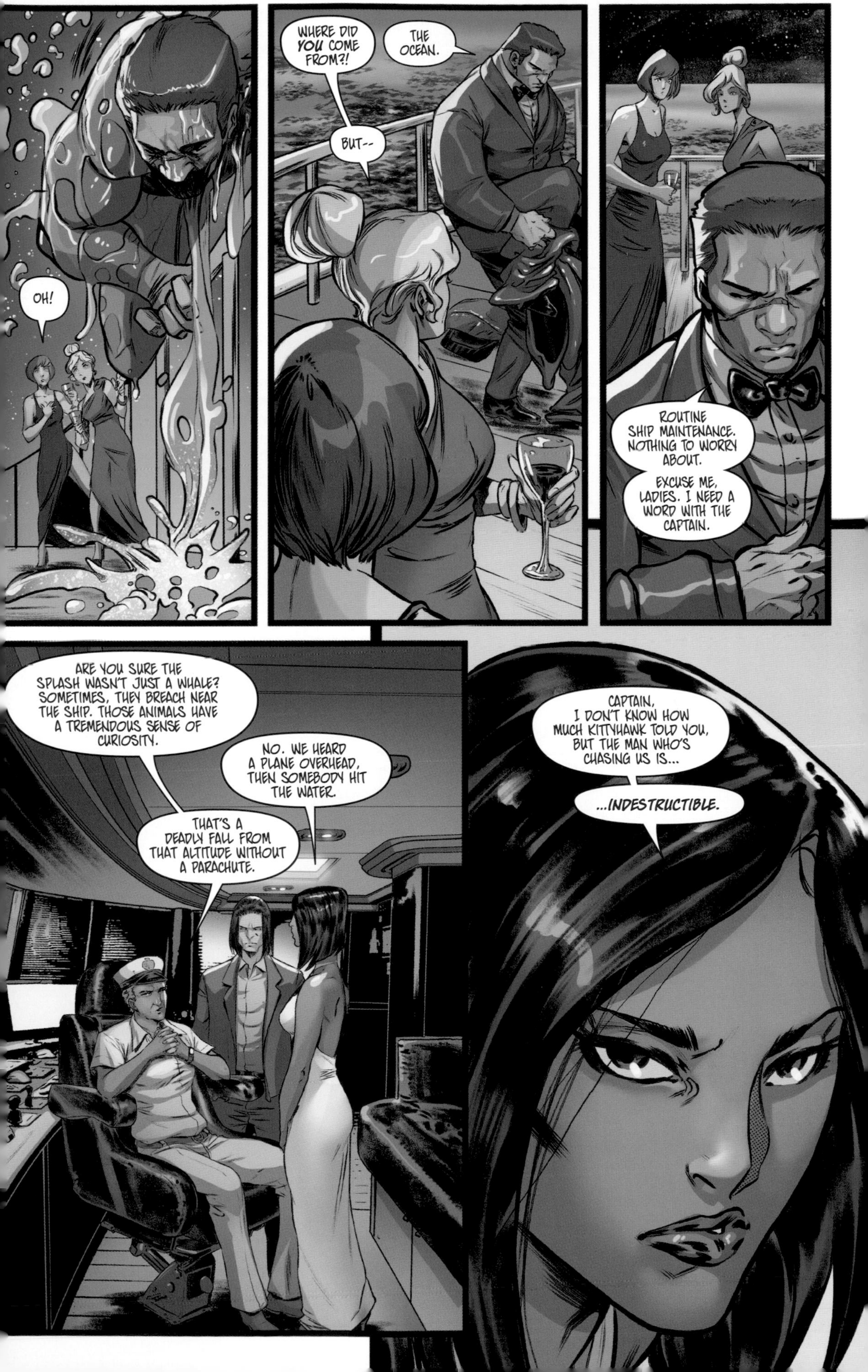
OH!
WHERE DID YOU COME FROM?!
THE OCEAN.
BUT--
ROUTINE SHIP MAINTENANCE. NOTHING TO WORRY ABOUT.
EXCUSE ME, LADIES. I NEED A WORD WITH THE CAPTAIN.
ARE YOU SURE THE SPLASH WASN'T JUST A WHALE? SOMETIMES, THEY BREACH NEAR THE SHIP. THOSE ANIMALS HAVE A TREMENDOUS SENSE OF CURIOSITY.
NO. WE HEARD A PLANE OVERHEAD, THEN SOMEBODY HIT THE WATER.
THAT'S A DEADLY FALL FROM THAT ALTITUDE WITHOUT A PARACHUTE.
CAPTAIN, I DON'T KNOW HOW MUCH KITTYHAWK TOLD YOU, BUT THE MAN WHO'S CHASING US IS...
...INDESTRUCTIBLE.

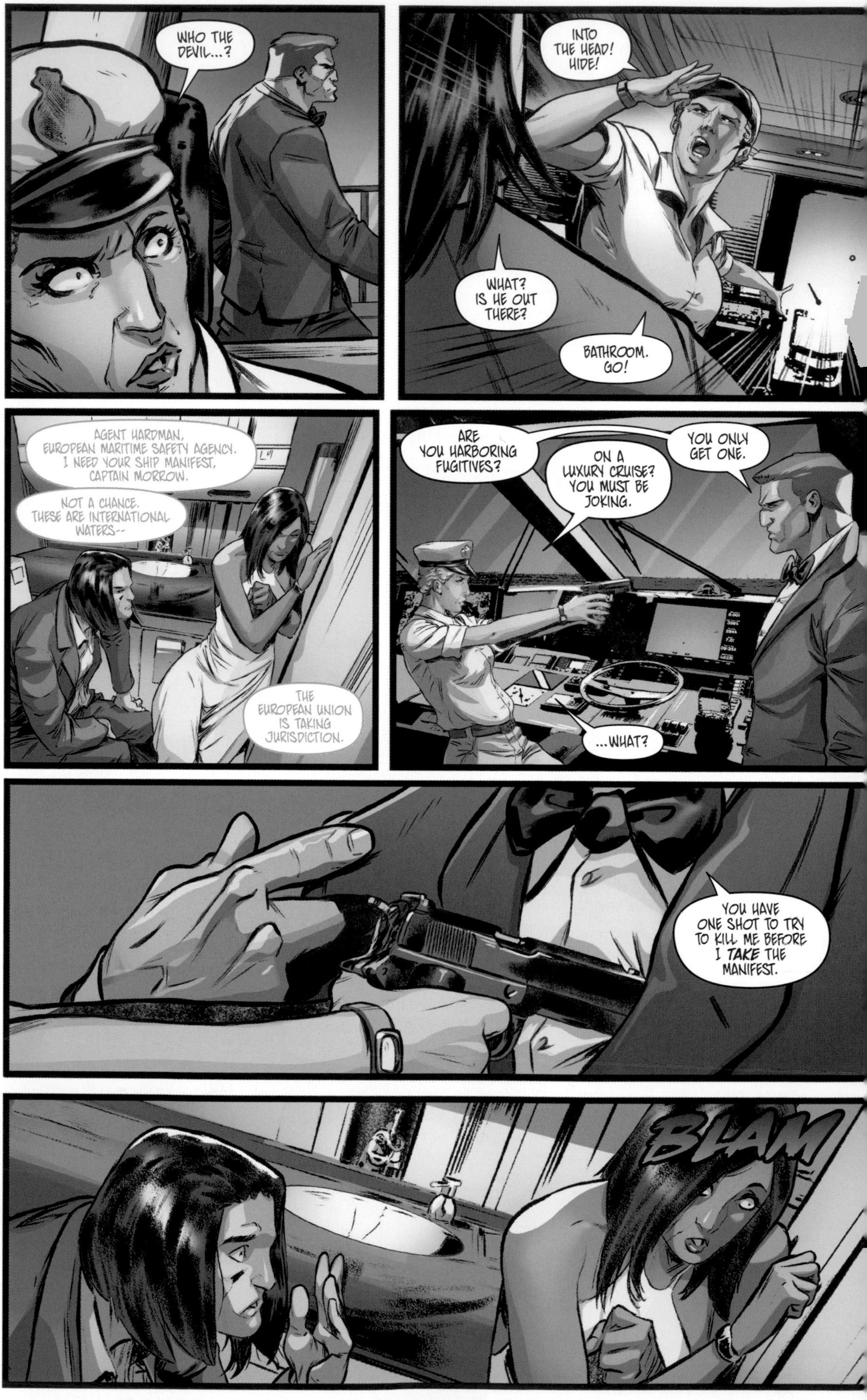
WHO THE DEVIL...?
INTO THE HEAD! HIDE!
WHAT? IS HE OUT THERE?
BATHROOM. GO!
AGENT HARDMAN, EUROPEAN MARITIME SAFETY AGENCY. I NEED YOUR SHIP MANIFEST, CAPTAIN MORROW.
NOT A CHANCE. THESE ARE INTERNATIONAL WATERS--
THE EUROPEAN UNION IS TAKING JURISDICTION.
ARE YOU HARBORING FUGITIVES?
ON A LUXURY CRUISE? YOU MUST BE JOKING.
YOU ONLY GET ONE.
...WHAT?
YOU HAVE ONE SHOT TO TRY TO KILL ME BEFORE I *TAKE* THE MANIFEST.
BLAM

I THINK HE'S GONE NOW. IT'S QUIET.

IF THAT... GARGOYLE...FINDS YOU ON MY SHIP, WE'RE ALL DEAD.

ANY LIFEBOATS?

USE THE STARBOARD INFLATABLE, AND HURRY. IT WON'T TAKE LONG FOR HIM TO CHECK ALL THE CABINS.

I'LL CHUCK IT OVERBOARD. YOU KEEP WATCH!

SOMEBODY'S COMING! HIDE!

CLK

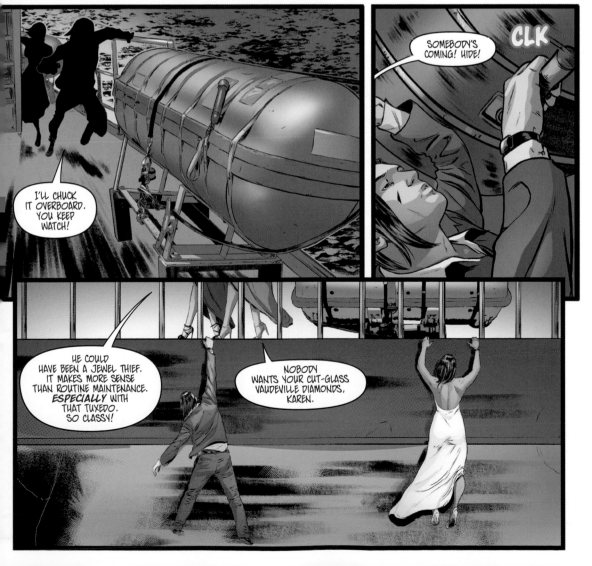

HE COULD HAVE BEEN A JEWEL THIEF. IT MAKES MORE SENSE THAN ROUTINE MAINTENANCE. *ESPECIALLY* WITH THAT TUXEDO. SO CLASSY!

NOBODY WANTS YOUR CUT-GLASS VAUDEVILLE DIAMONDS, KAREN.

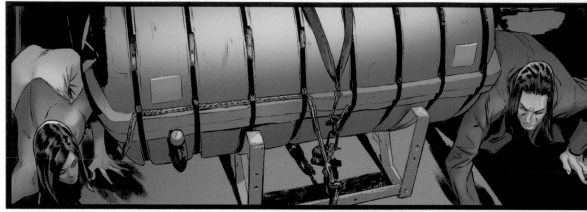

SPASH

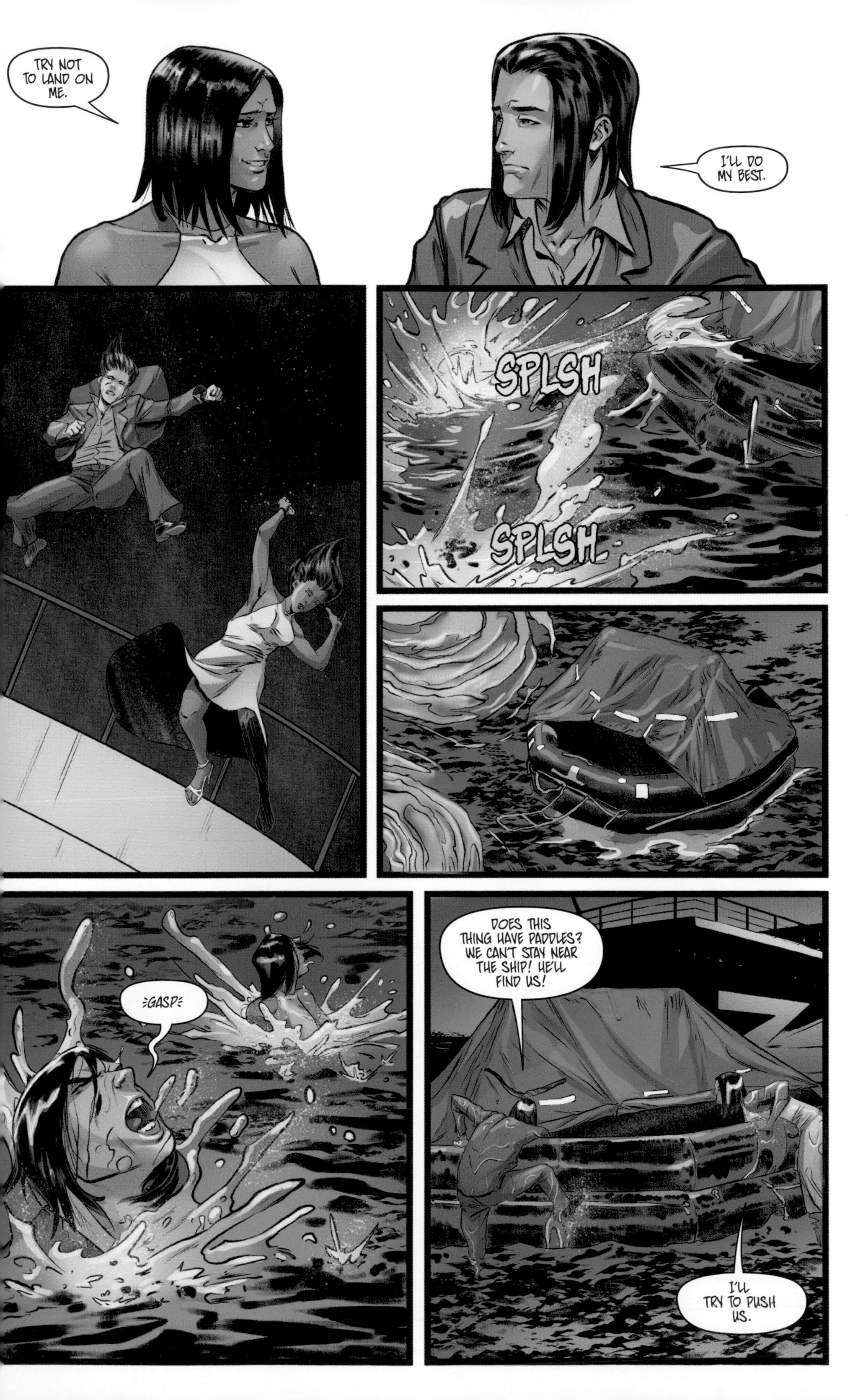
TRY NOT TO LAND ON ME.
I'LL DO MY BEST.
SPLSH
SPLSH
GASP
DOES THIS THING HAVE PADDLES? WE CAN'T STAY NEAR THE SHIP! HE'LL FIND US!
I'LL TRY TO PUSH US.

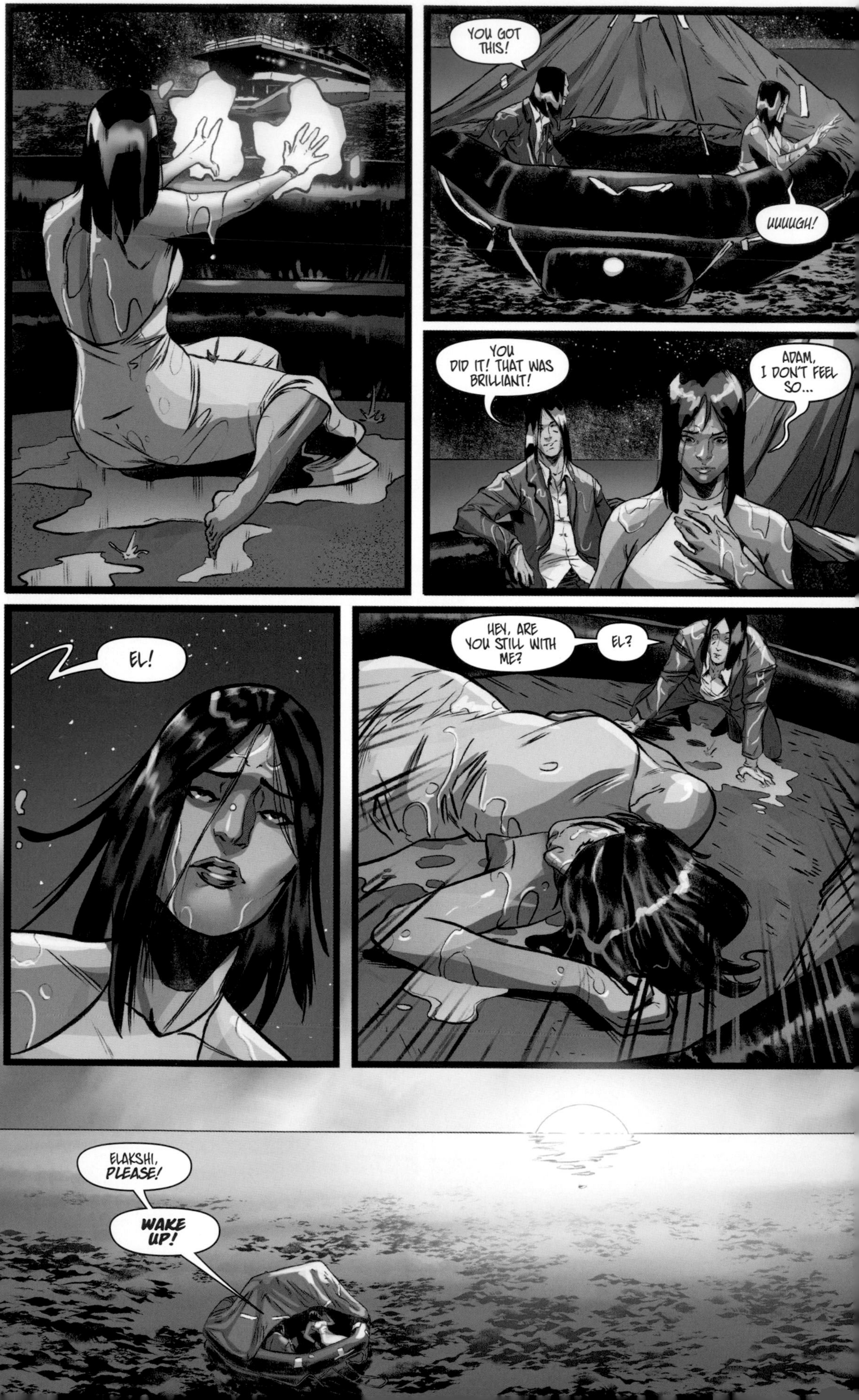
YOU GOT THIS!
UUUUGH!
YOU DID IT! THAT WAS BRILLIANT!
ADAM, I DON'T FEEL SO...
EL!
HEY, ARE YOU STILL WITH ME?
EL?
ELAKSHI, PLEASE!
WAKE UP!

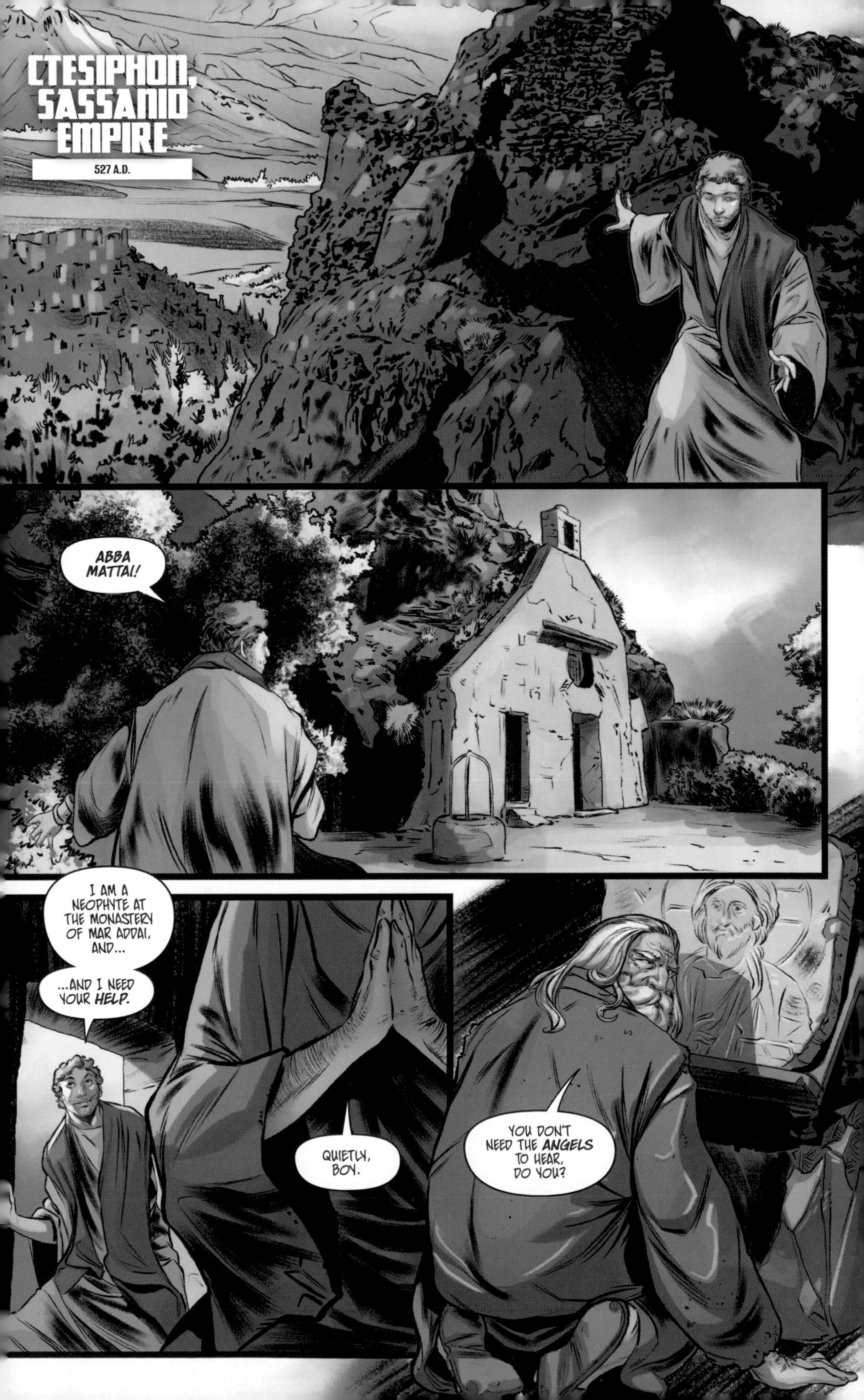
CTESIPHON, SASSANID EMPIRE
527 A.D.
ABBA MATTAI!
I AM A NEOPHYTE AT THE MONASTERY OF MAR ADDAI, AND...
...AND I NEED YOUR HELP.
QUIETLY, BOY.
YOU DON'T NEED THE ANGELS TO HEAR, DO YOU?

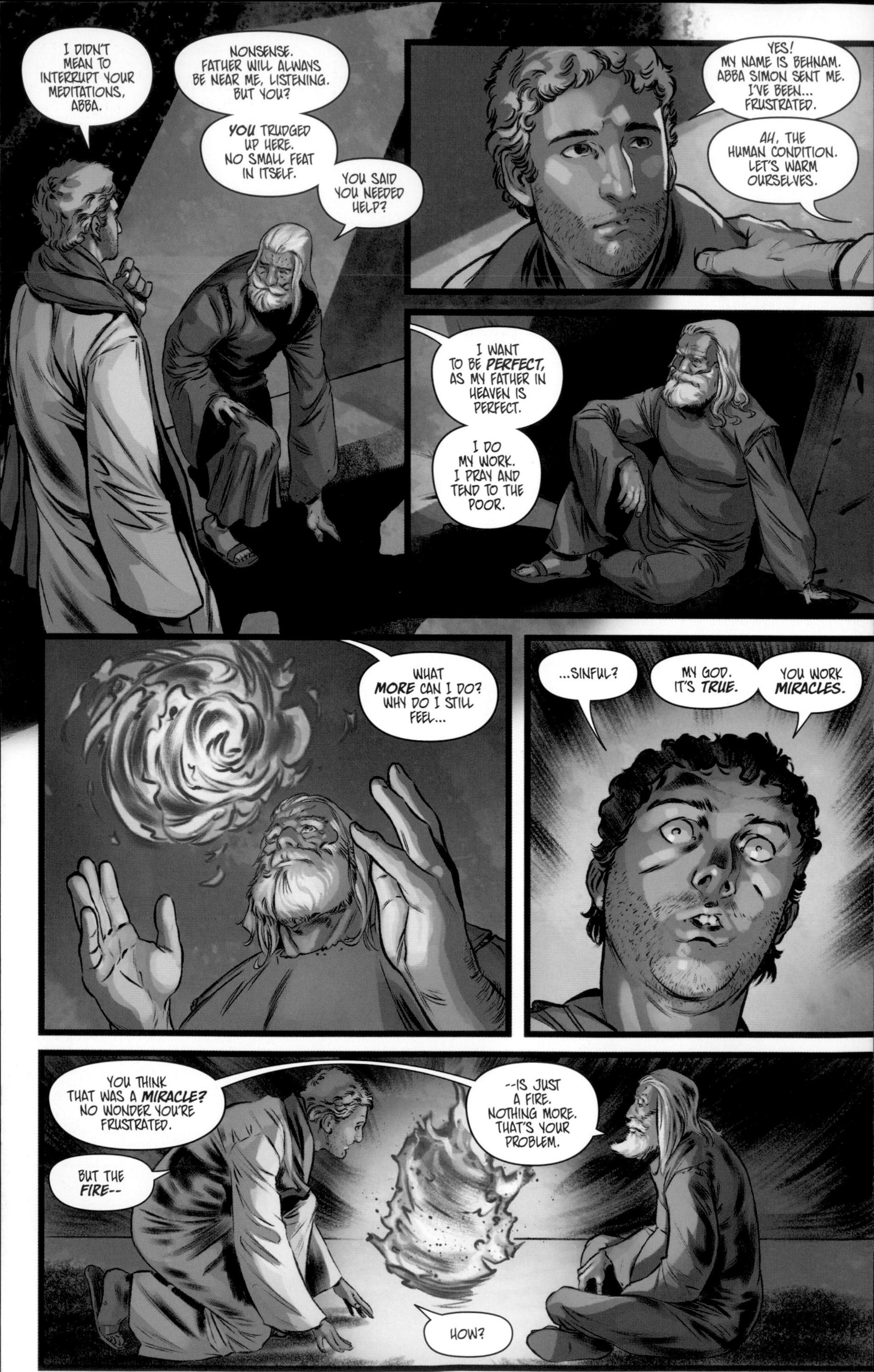
I DIDN'T MEAN TO INTERRUPT YOUR MEDITATIONS, ABBA.
NONSENSE. FATHER WILL ALWAYS BE NEAR ME, LISTENING. BUT YOU?
YOU TRUDGED UP HERE. NO SMALL FEAT IN ITSELF.
YOU SAID YOU NEEDED HELP?
YES! MY NAME IS BEHNAM. ABBA SIMON SENT ME. I'VE BEEN... FRUSTRATED.
AH, THE HUMAN CONDITION. LET'S WARM OURSELVES.
I WANT TO BE PERFECT, AS MY FATHER IN HEAVEN IS PERFECT.
I DO MY WORK. I PRAY AND TEND TO THE POOR.
WHAT MORE CAN I DO? WHY DO I STILL FEEL...
...SINFUL?
MY GOD. IT'S TRUE.
YOU WORK MIRACLES.
YOU THINK THAT WAS A MIRACLE? NO WONDER YOU'RE FRUSTRATED.
BUT THE FIRE--
--IS JUST A FIRE. NOTHING MORE. THAT'S YOUR PROBLEM.
HOW?

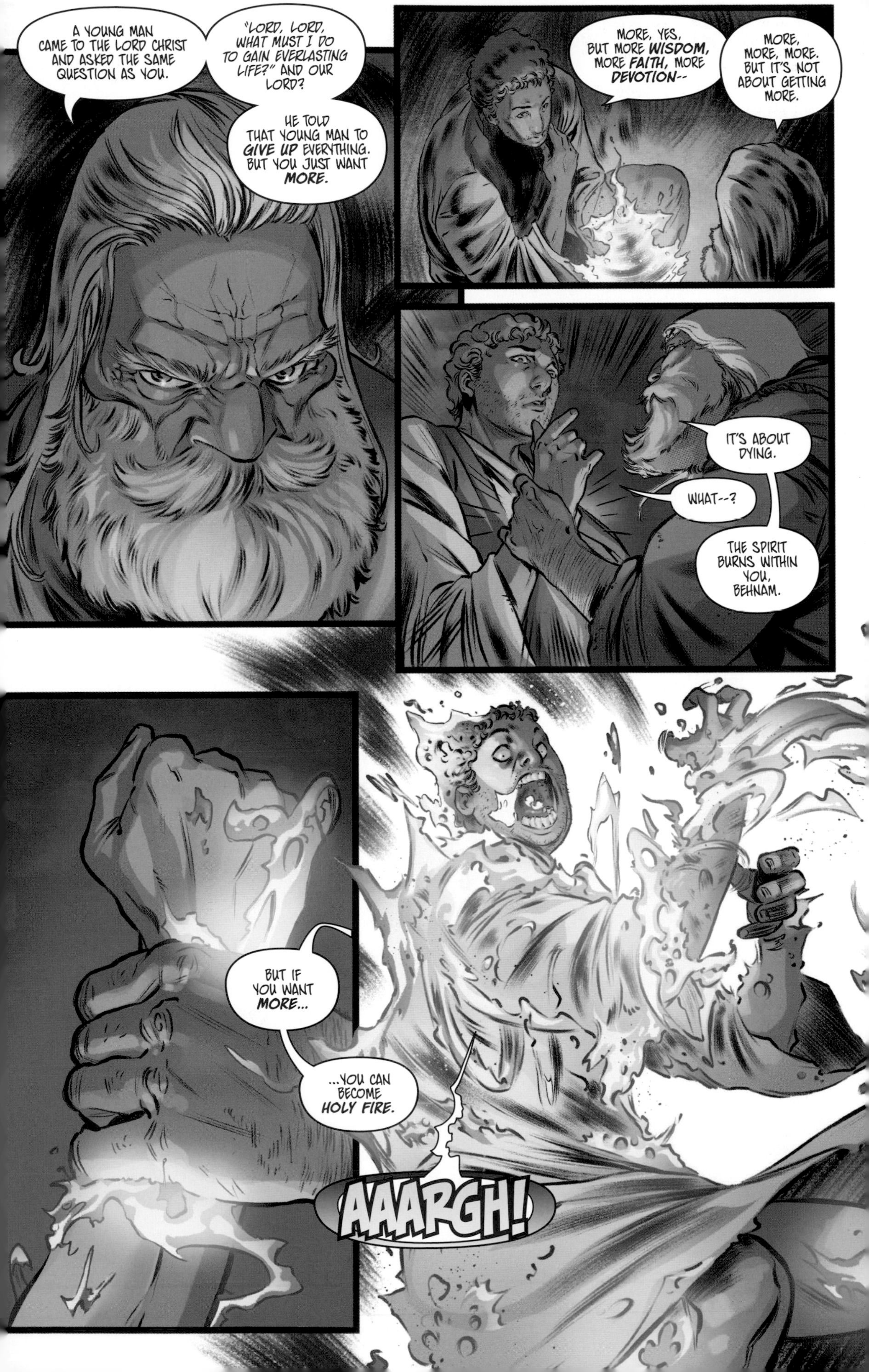
A YOUNG MAN CAME TO THE LORD CHRIST AND ASKED THE SAME QUESTION AS YOU.
"LORD, LORD, WHAT MUST I DO TO GAIN EVERLASTING LIFE?" AND OUR LORD?
HE TOLD THAT YOUNG MAN TO GIVE UP EVERYTHING. BUT YOU JUST WANT MORE.
MORE, YES, BUT MORE WISDOM, MORE FAITH, MORE DEVOTION--
MORE, MORE, MORE. BUT IT'S NOT ABOUT GETTING MORE.
IT'S ABOUT DYING.
WHAT--?
THE SPIRIT BURNS WITHIN YOU, BEHNAM.
BUT IF YOU WANT MORE...
...YOU CAN BECOME HOLY FIRE.
AAARGH!

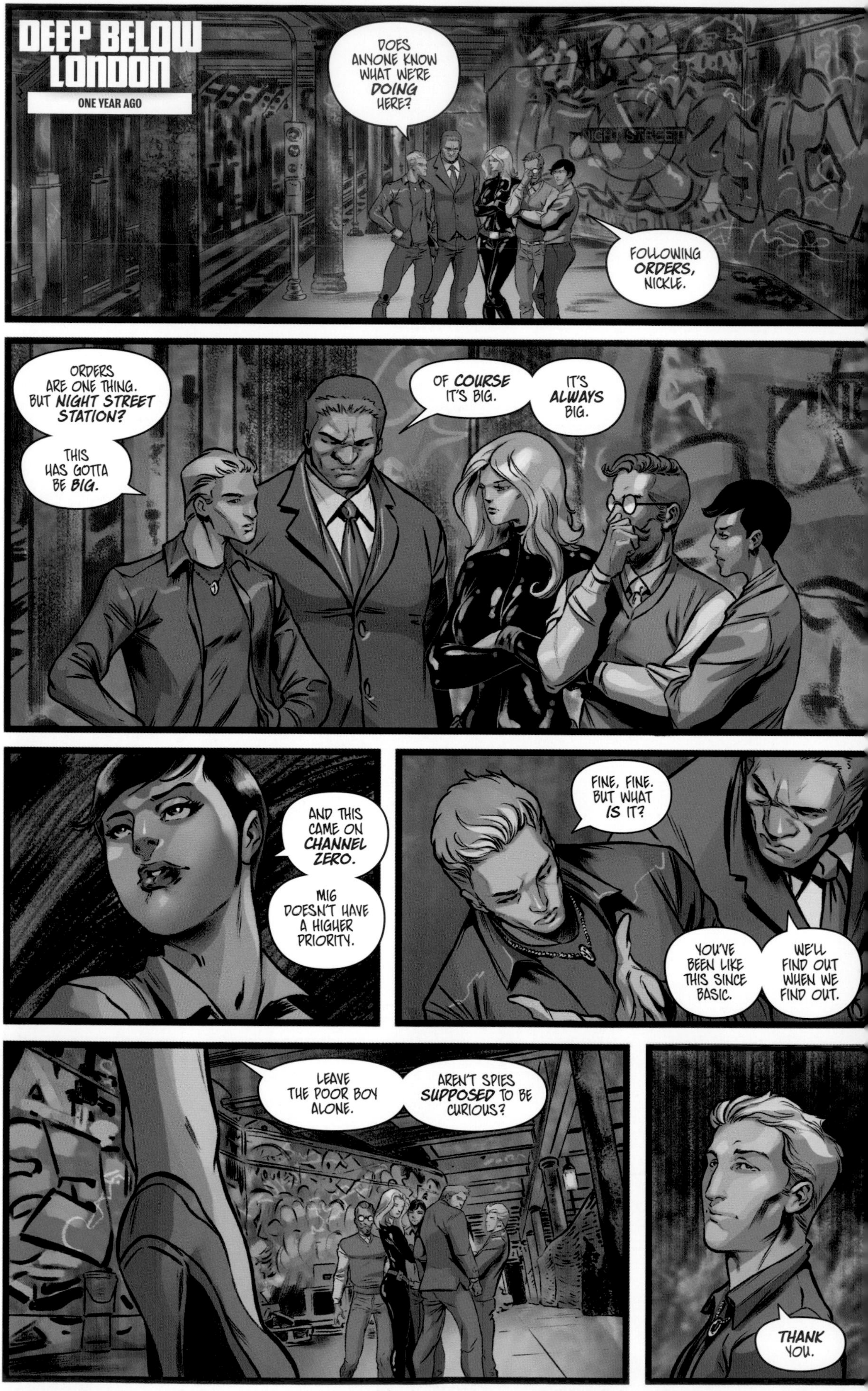
DEEP BELOW LONDON
ONE YEAR AGO
DOES ANYONE KNOW WHAT WE'RE DOING HERE?
NIGHT STREET
FOLLOWING ORDERS, NICKLE.
ORDERS ARE ONE THING. BUT NIGHT STREET STATION?
THIS HAS GOTTA BE BIG.
OF COURSE IT'S BIG.
IT'S ALWAYS BIG.
AND THIS CAME ON CHANNEL ZERO.
MI6 DOESN'T HAVE A HIGHER PRIORITY.
FINE, FINE. BUT WHAT IS IT?
YOU'VE BEEN LIKE THIS SINCE BASIC.
WE'LL FIND OUT WHEN WE FIND OUT.
LEAVE THE POOR BOY ALONE.
AREN'T SPIES SUPPOSED TO BE CURIOUS?
THANK YOU.

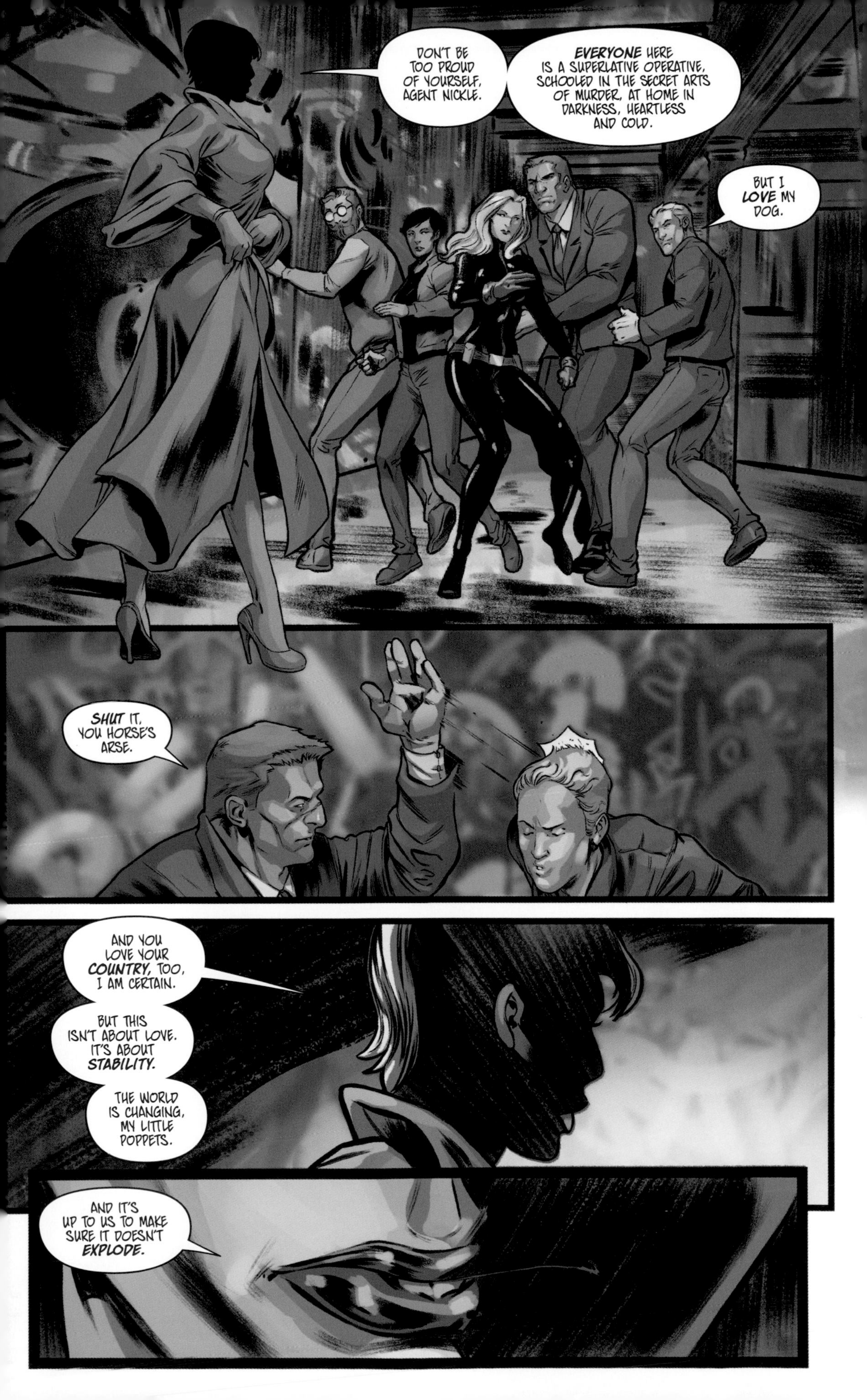
DON'T BE TOO PROUD OF YOURSELF, AGENT NICKLE.
EVERYONE HERE IS A SUPERLATIVE OPERATIVE, SCHOOLED IN THE SECRET ARTS OF MURDER, AT HOME IN DARKNESS, HEARTLESS AND COLD.
BUT I LOVE MY DOG.
SHUT IT, YOU HORSE'S ARSE.
AND YOU LOVE YOUR COUNTRY, TOO, I AM CERTAIN.
BUT THIS ISN'T ABOUT LOVE. IT'S ABOUT STABILITY.
THE WORLD IS CHANGING, MY LITTLE POPPETS.
AND IT'S UP TO US TO MAKE SURE IT DOESN'T EXPLODE.

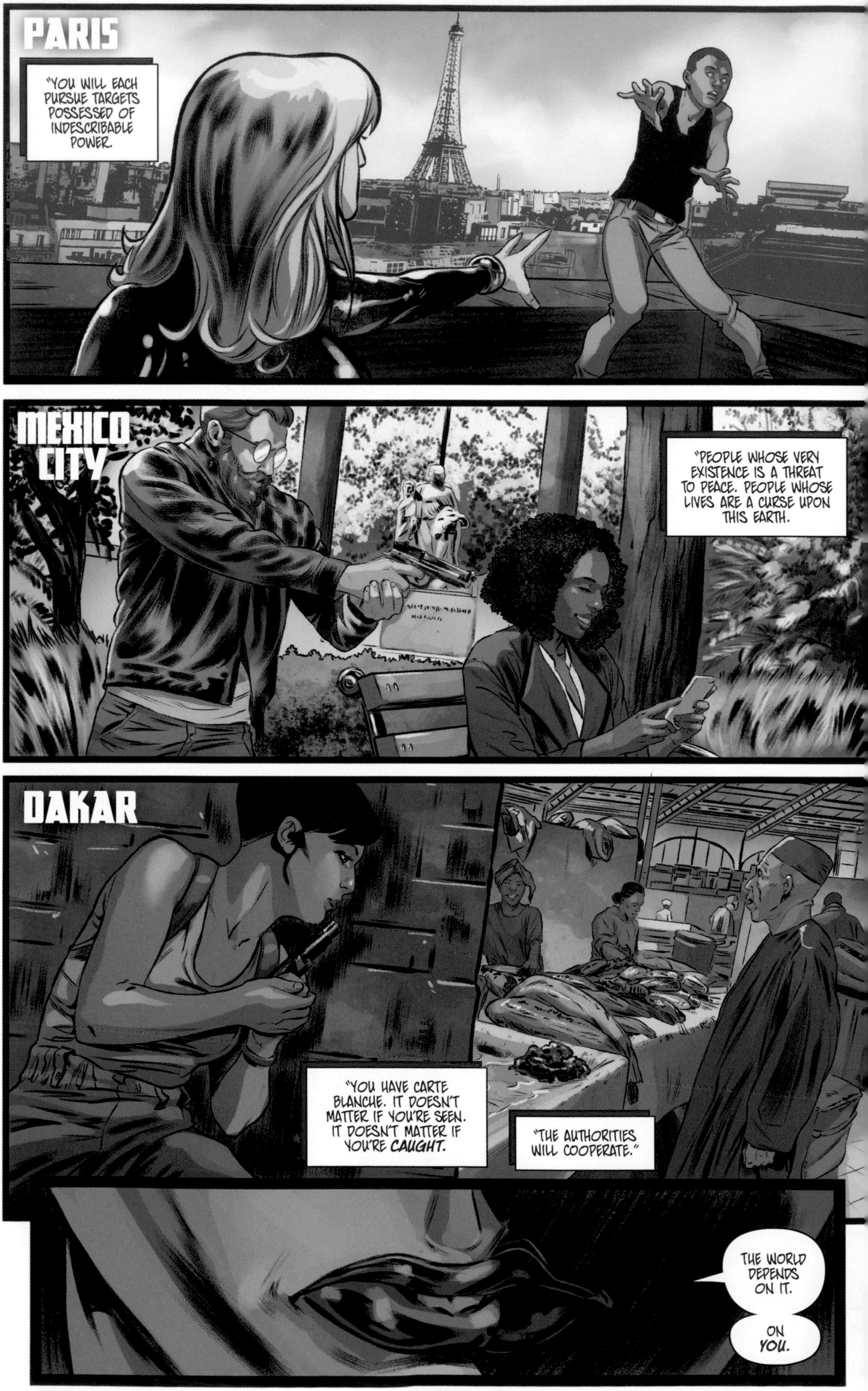
PARIS
"YOU WILL EACH PURSUE TARGETS POSSESSED OF INDESCRIBABLE POWER.
MEXICO CITY
"PEOPLE WHOSE VERY EXISTENCE IS A THREAT TO PEACE. PEOPLE WHOSE LIVES ARE A CURSE UPON THIS EARTH.
DAKAR
"YOU HAVE CARTE BLANCHE. IT DOESN'T MATTER IF YOU'RE SEEN. IT DOESN'T MATTER IF YOU'RE CAUGHT.
"THE AUTHORITIES WILL COOPERATE."
THE WORLD DEPENDS ON IT.
ON YOU.

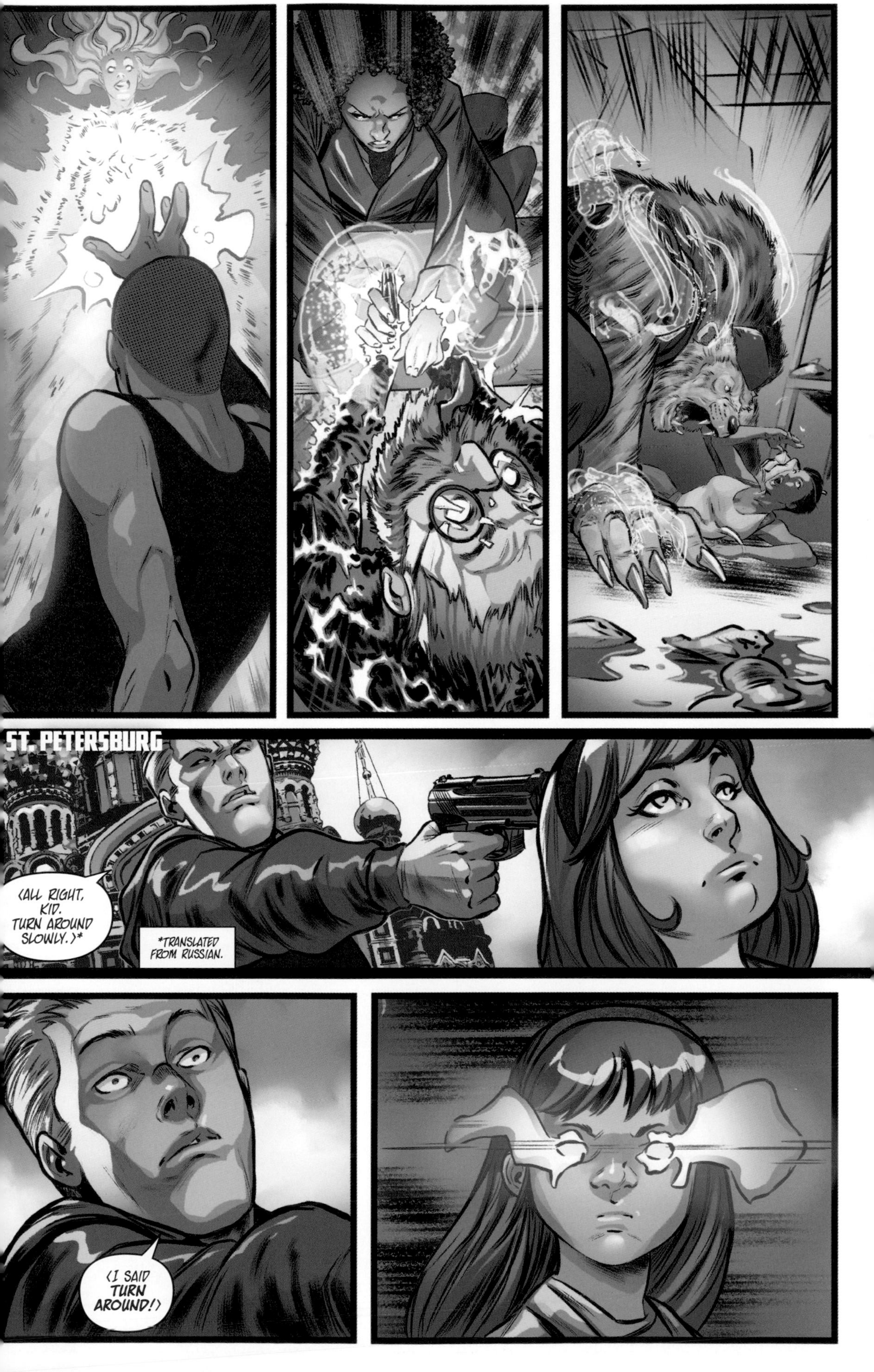
ST. PETERSBURG
‹ALL RIGHT, KID. TURN AROUND SLOWLY.›*
*TRANSLATED FROM RUSSIAN.
‹I SAID TURN AROUND!›

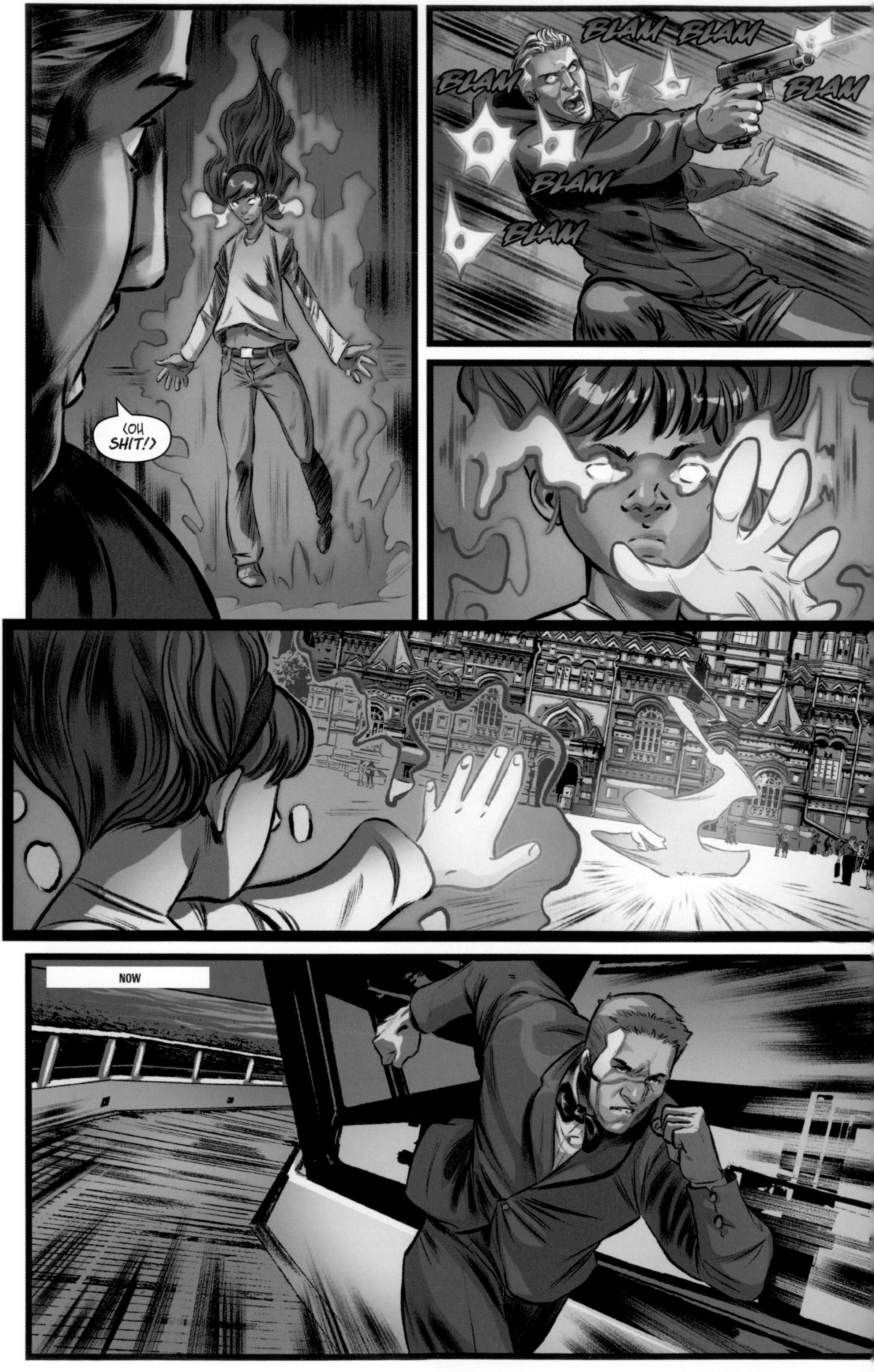
‹OH SHIT!›
BLAM BLAM
BLAM
BLAM
BLAM
BLAM
NOW

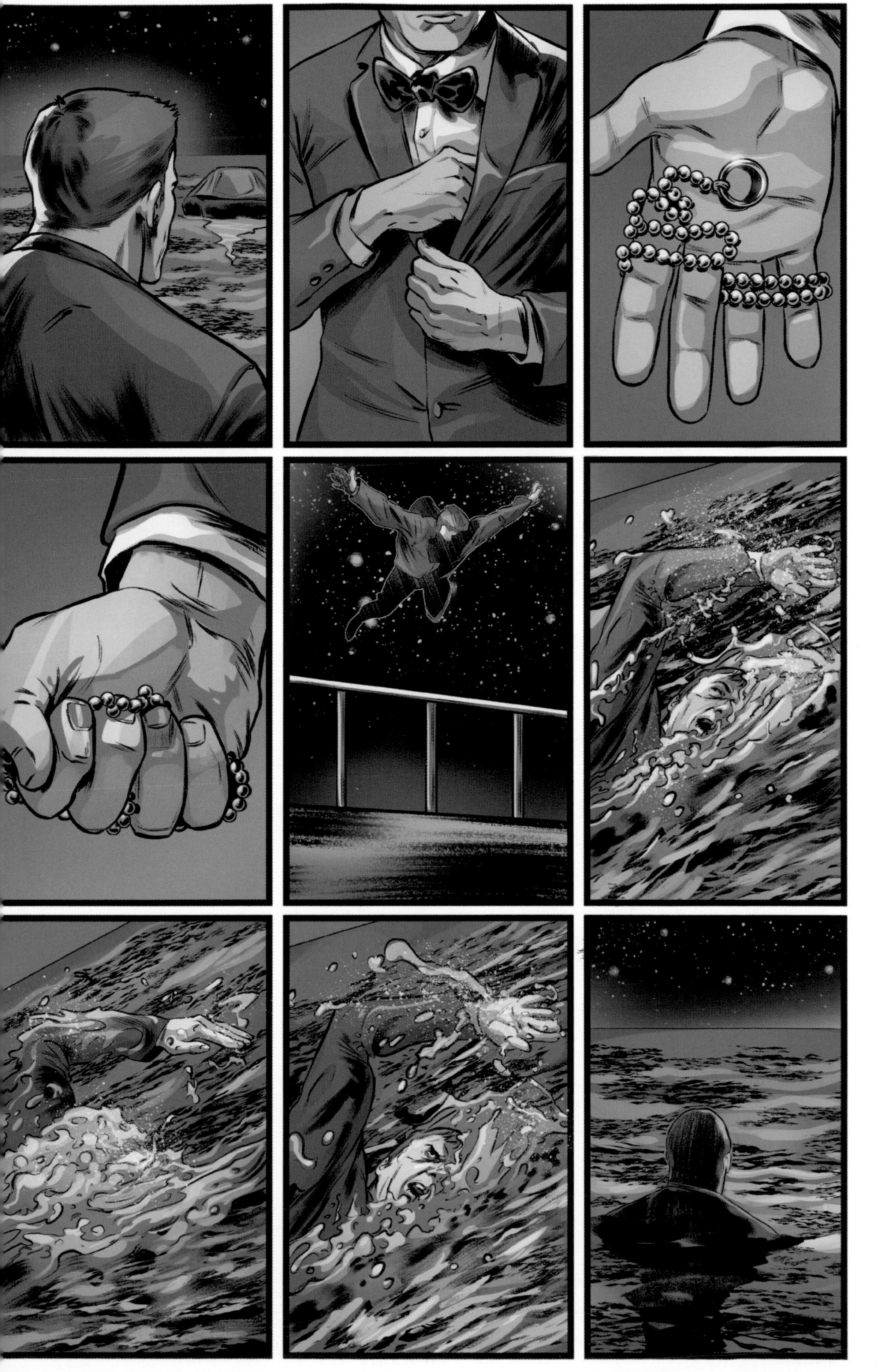

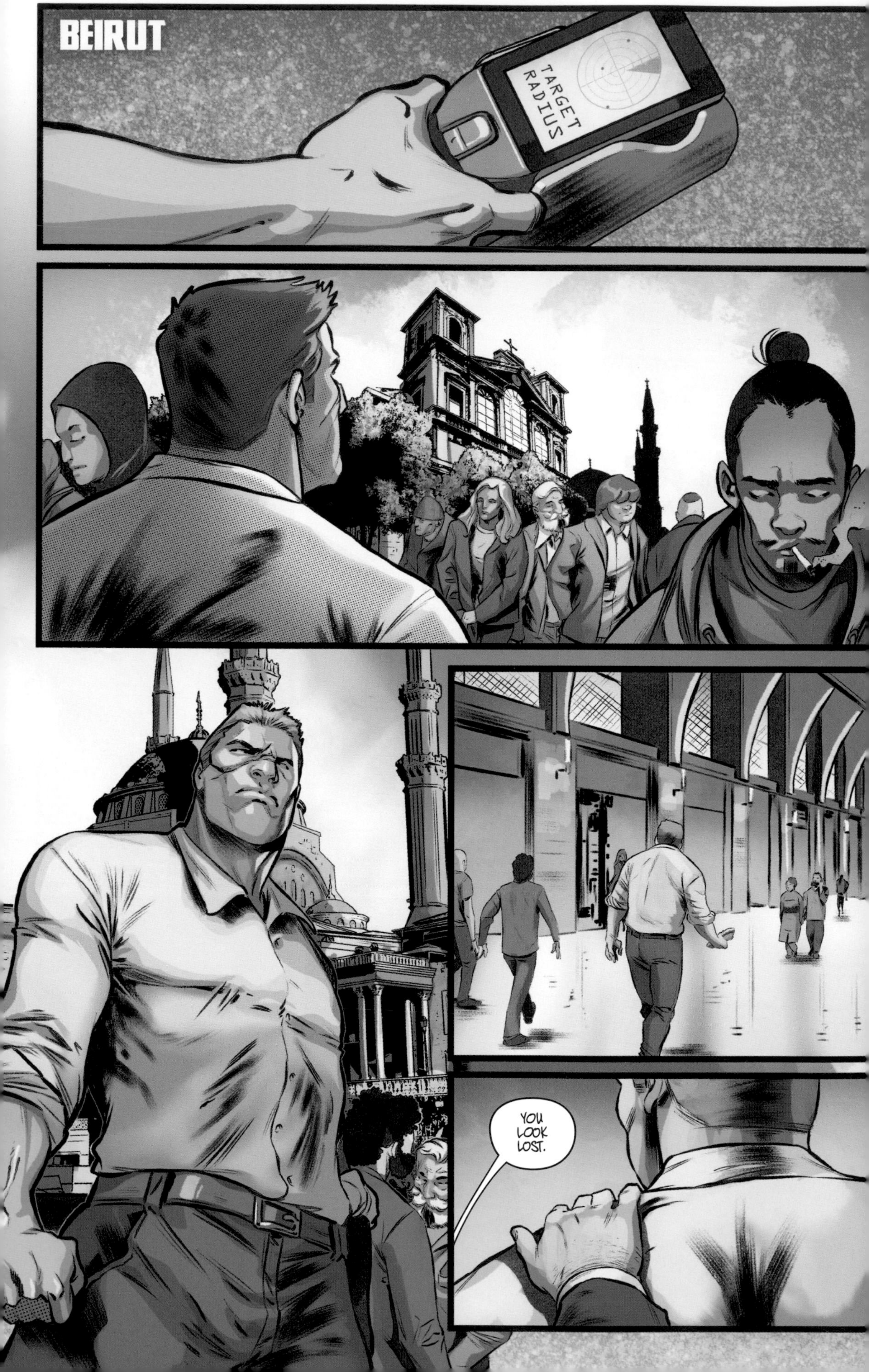
BEIRUT
TARGET RADIUS
YOU LOOK LOST.

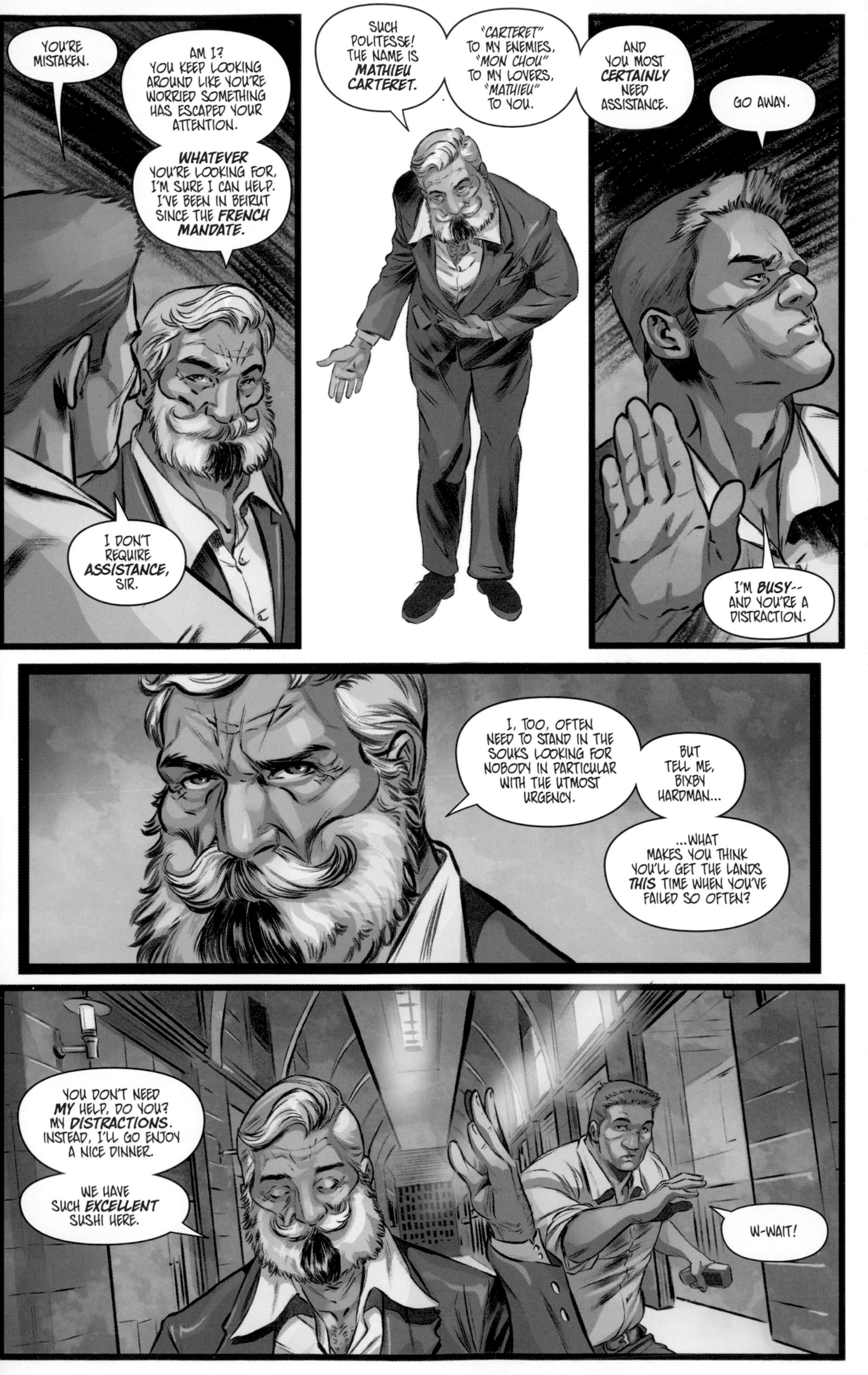
YOU'RE MISTAKEN.
AM I? YOU KEEP LOOKING AROUND LIKE YOU'RE WORRIED SOMETHING HAS ESCAPED YOUR ATTENTION.
WHATEVER YOU'RE LOOKING FOR, I'M SURE I CAN HELP. I'VE BEEN IN BEIRUT SINCE THE FRENCH MANDATE.
I DON'T REQUIRE ASSISTANCE, SIR.
SUCH POLITESSE! THE NAME IS MATHIEU CARTERET.
"CARTERET" TO MY ENEMIES, "MON CHOU" TO MY LOVERS, "MATHIEU" TO YOU.
AND YOU MOST CERTAINLY NEED ASSISTANCE.
GO AWAY.
I'M BUSY-- AND YOU'RE A DISTRACTION.
I, TOO, OFTEN NEED TO STAND IN THE SOUKS LOOKING FOR NOBODY IN PARTICULAR WITH THE UTMOST URGENCY.
BUT TELL ME, BIXBY HARDMAN...
...WHAT MAKES YOU THINK YOU'LL GET THE LANDS THIS TIME WHEN YOU'VE FAILED SO OFTEN?
YOU DON'T NEED MY HELP, DO YOU? MY DISTRACTIONS. INSTEAD, I'LL GO ENJOY A NICE DINNER.
WE HAVE SUCH EXCELLENT SUSHI HERE.
W-WAIT!

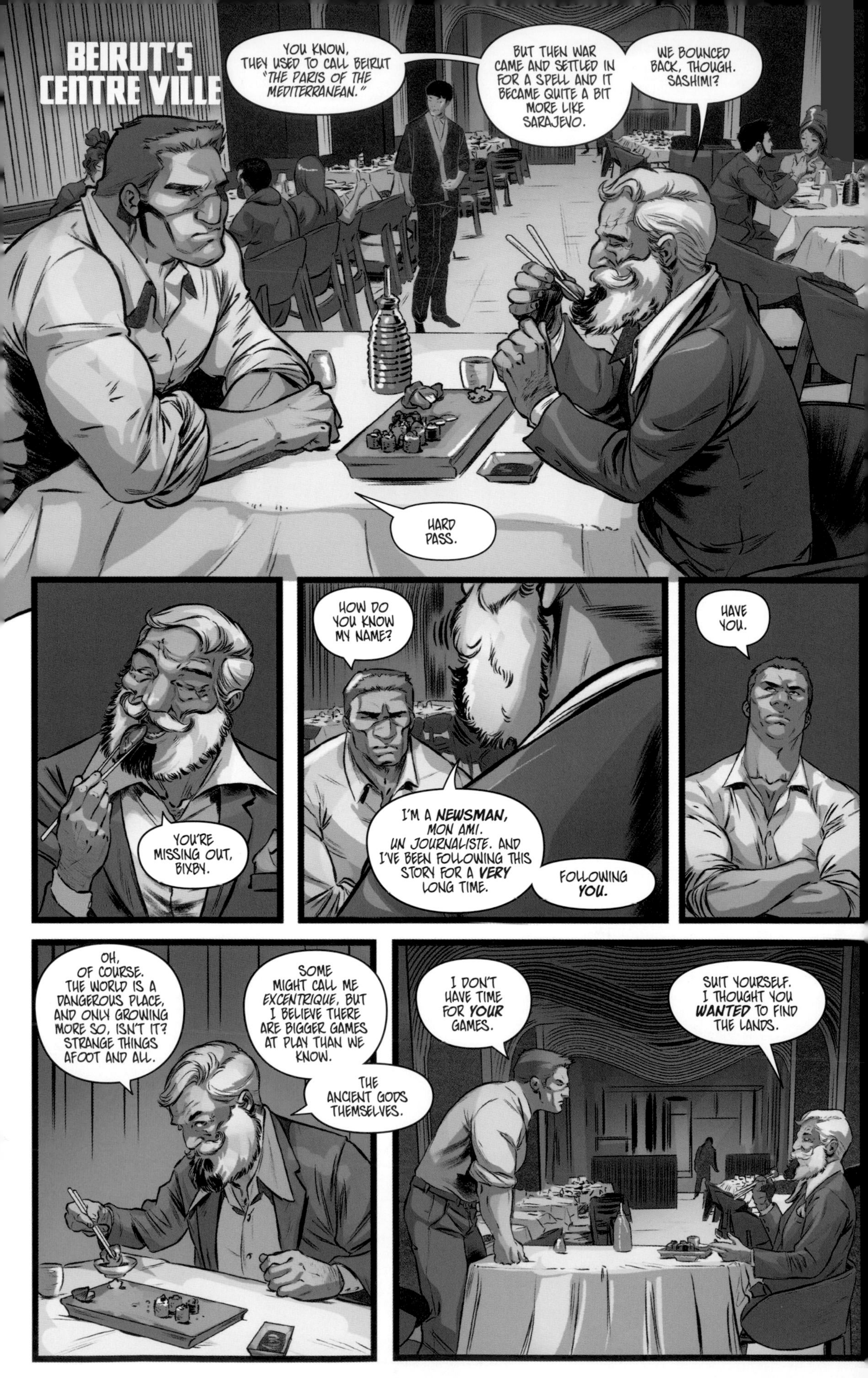
BEIRUT'S CENTRE VILLE
YOU KNOW, THEY USED TO CALL BEIRUT "THE PARIS OF THE MEDITERRANEAN."
BUT THEN WAR CAME AND SETTLED IN FOR A SPELL AND IT BECAME QUITE A BIT MORE LIKE SARAJEVO.
WE BOUNCED BACK, THOUGH. SASHIMI?
HARD PASS.
YOU'RE MISSING OUT, BIXBY.
HOW DO YOU KNOW MY NAME?
I'M A NEWSMAN, MON AMI. UN JOURNALISTE. AND I'VE BEEN FOLLOWING THIS STORY FOR A VERY LONG TIME.
FOLLOWING YOU.
HAVE YOU.
OH, OF COURSE. THE WORLD IS A DANGEROUS PLACE, AND ONLY GROWING MORE SO, ISN'T IT? STRANGE THINGS AFOOT AND ALL.
SOME MIGHT CALL ME EXCENTRIQUE, BUT I BELIEVE THERE ARE BIGGER GAMES AT PLAY THAN WE KNOW.
THE ANCIENT GODS THEMSELVES.
I DON'T HAVE TIME FOR YOUR GAMES.
SUIT YOURSELF. I THOUGHT YOU WANTED TO FIND THE LANDS.

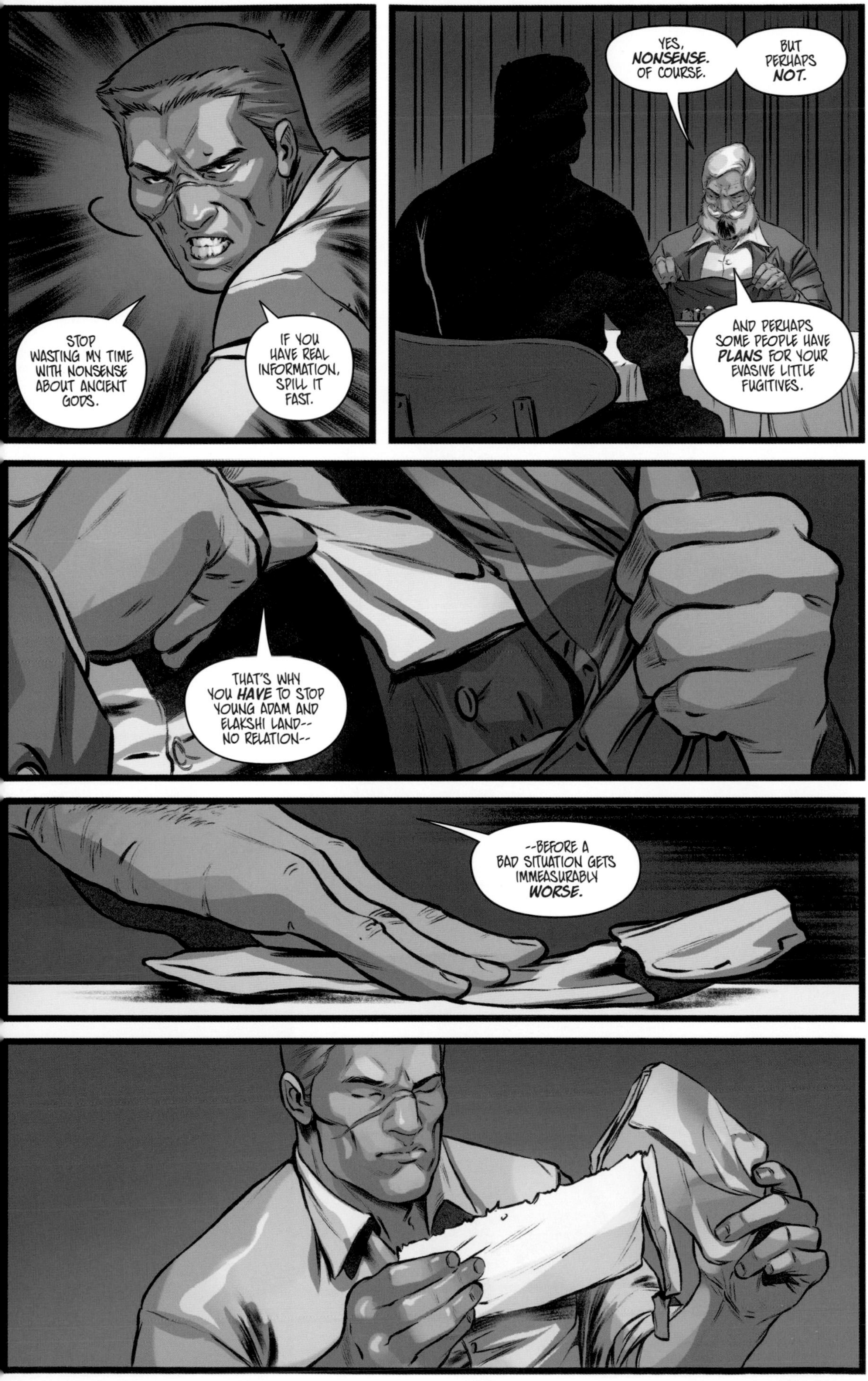
STOP WASTING MY TIME WITH NONSENSE ABOUT ANCIENT GODS.
IF YOU HAVE REAL INFORMATION, SPILL IT FAST.
YES, NONSENSE. OF COURSE.
BUT PERHAPS NOT.
AND PERHAPS SOME PEOPLE HAVE PLANS FOR YOUR EVASIVE LITTLE FUGITIVES.
THAT'S WHY YOU HAVE TO STOP YOUNG ADAM AND ELAKSHI LAND-- NO RELATION--
--BEFORE A BAD SITUATION GETS IMMEASURABLY WORSE.

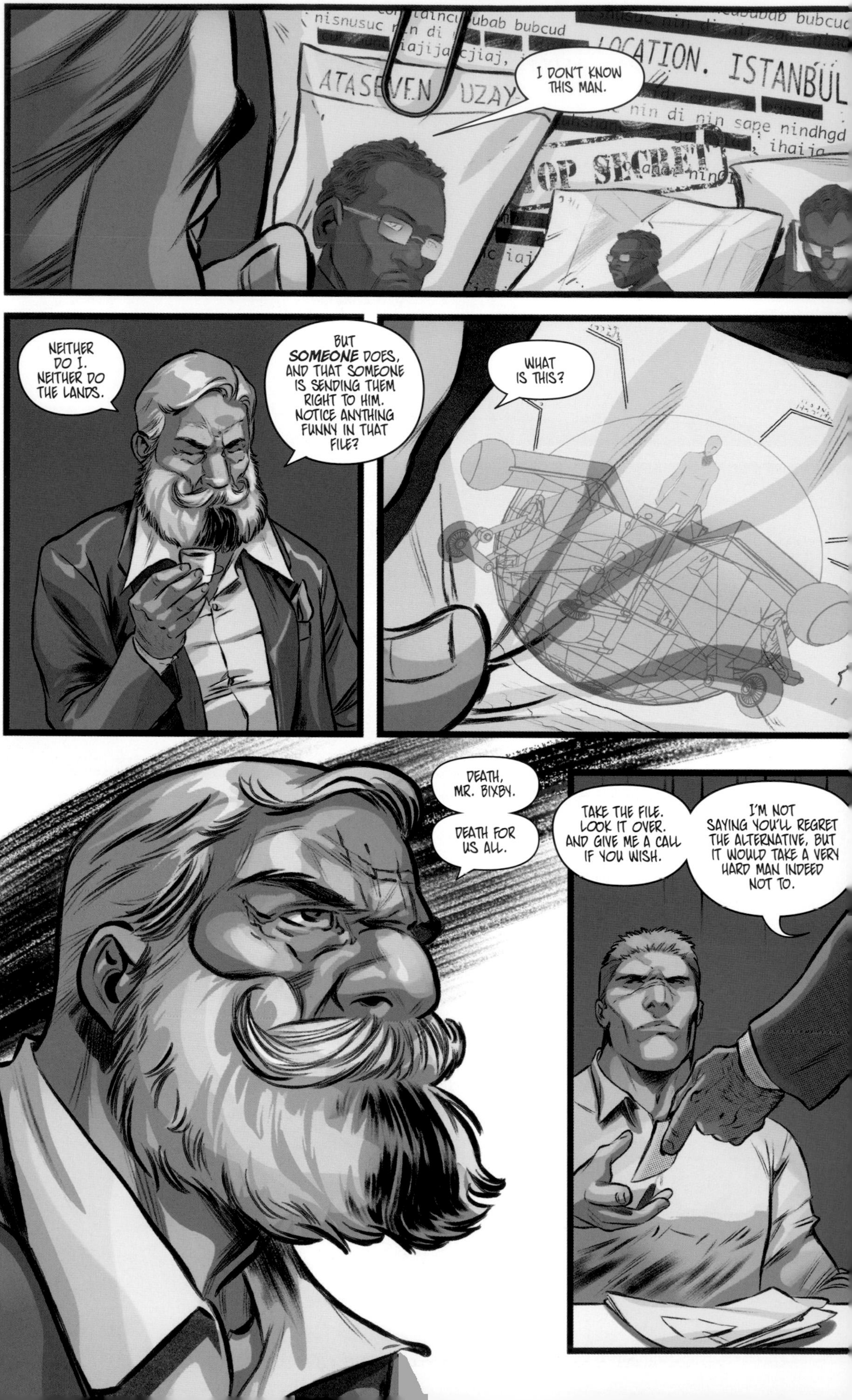
I DON'T KNOW THIS MAN.
NEITHER DO I. NEITHER DO THE LANDS.
BUT SOMEONE DOES, AND THAT SOMEONE IS SENDING THEM RIGHT TO HIM. NOTICE ANYTHING FUNNY IN THAT FILE?
WHAT IS THIS?
DEATH, MR. BIXBY.
DEATH FOR US ALL.
TAKE THE FILE. LOOK IT OVER. AND GIVE ME A CALL IF YOU WISH.
I'M NOT SAYING YOU'LL REGRET THE ALTERNATIVE, BUT IT WOULD TAKE A VERY HARD MAN INDEED NOT TO.

I HAVE A RESERVATION.

IT'S UNDER **HARCOURT FENTON.**

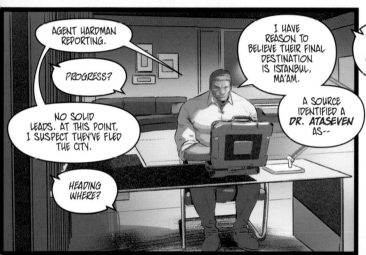

AGENT HARDMAN REPORTING.

PROGRESS?

NO SOLID LEADS. AT THIS POINT, I SUSPECT THEY'VE FLED THE CITY.

HEADING WHERE?

I HAVE REASON TO BELIEVE THEIR FINAL DESTINATION IS ISTANBUL, MA'AM.

A SOURCE IDENTIFIED A **DR. ATASEVEN** AS--

DISREGARD ANY LEADS REGARDING UZAY ATASEVEN.

I DON'T UNDERSTAND. IF THIS PANS OUT--

THAT IS A DEAD LEAD. HE HAS BEEN INVESTIGATED.

ACCORDING TO MY SOURCE, PURSUING THE DR. ATASEVEN ANGLE COULD UNRAVEL--

YOUR TARGETS ARE THE **LANDS.** STAY FOCUSED. YOU ARE UNDER ORDERS.

END TRANSMISSION.

Hamza Street 19:00 Tomorrow

MATHIEU CARTERET

- MAN OF SUBSTANCE

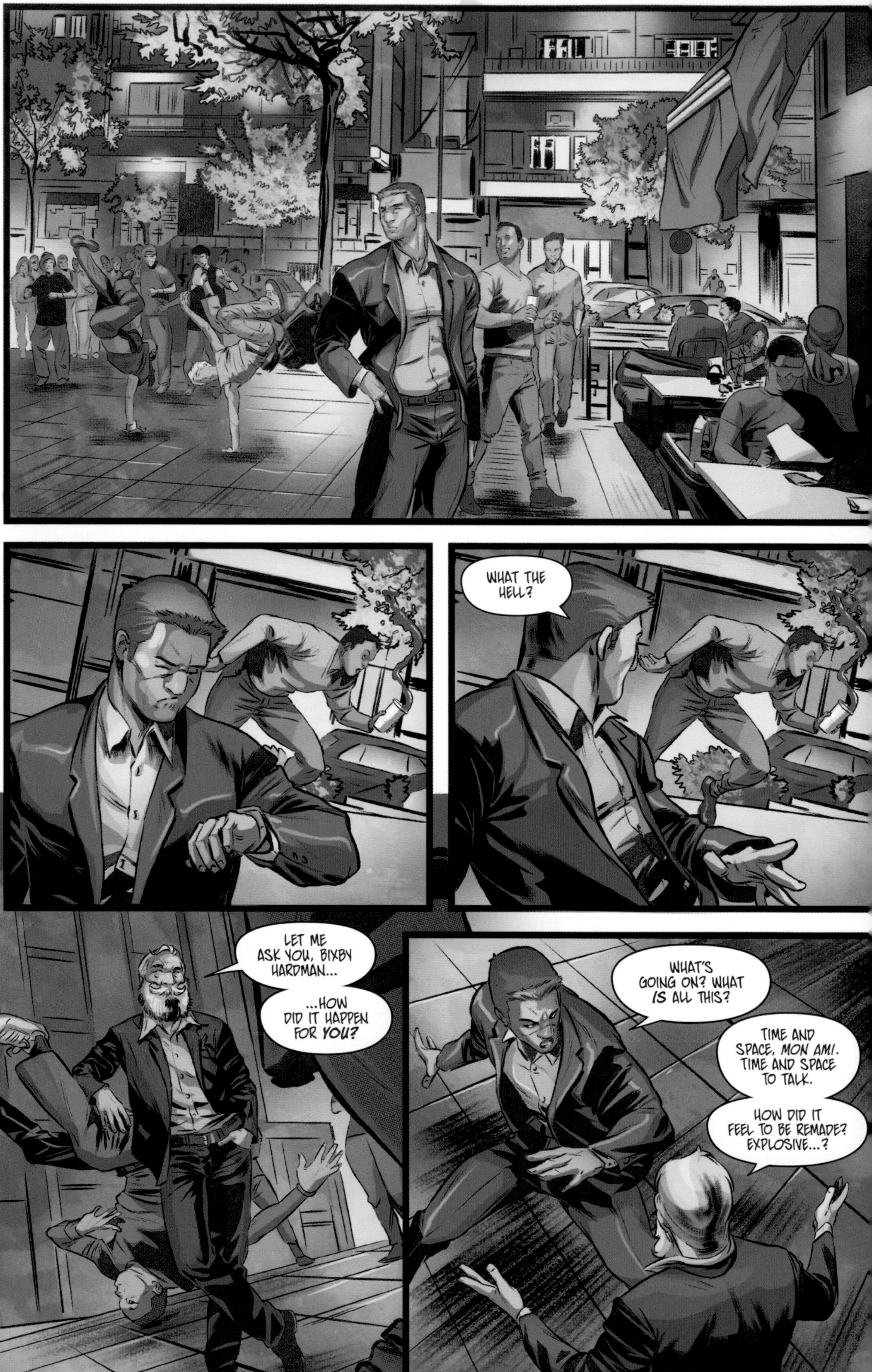
WHAT THE HELL?
LET ME ASK YOU, BIXBY HARDMAN...
...HOW DID IT HAPPEN FOR YOU?
WHAT'S GOING ON? WHAT IS ALL THIS?
TIME AND SPACE, MON AMI. TIME AND SPACE TO TALK.
HOW DID IT FEEL TO BE REMADE? EXPLOSIVE...?

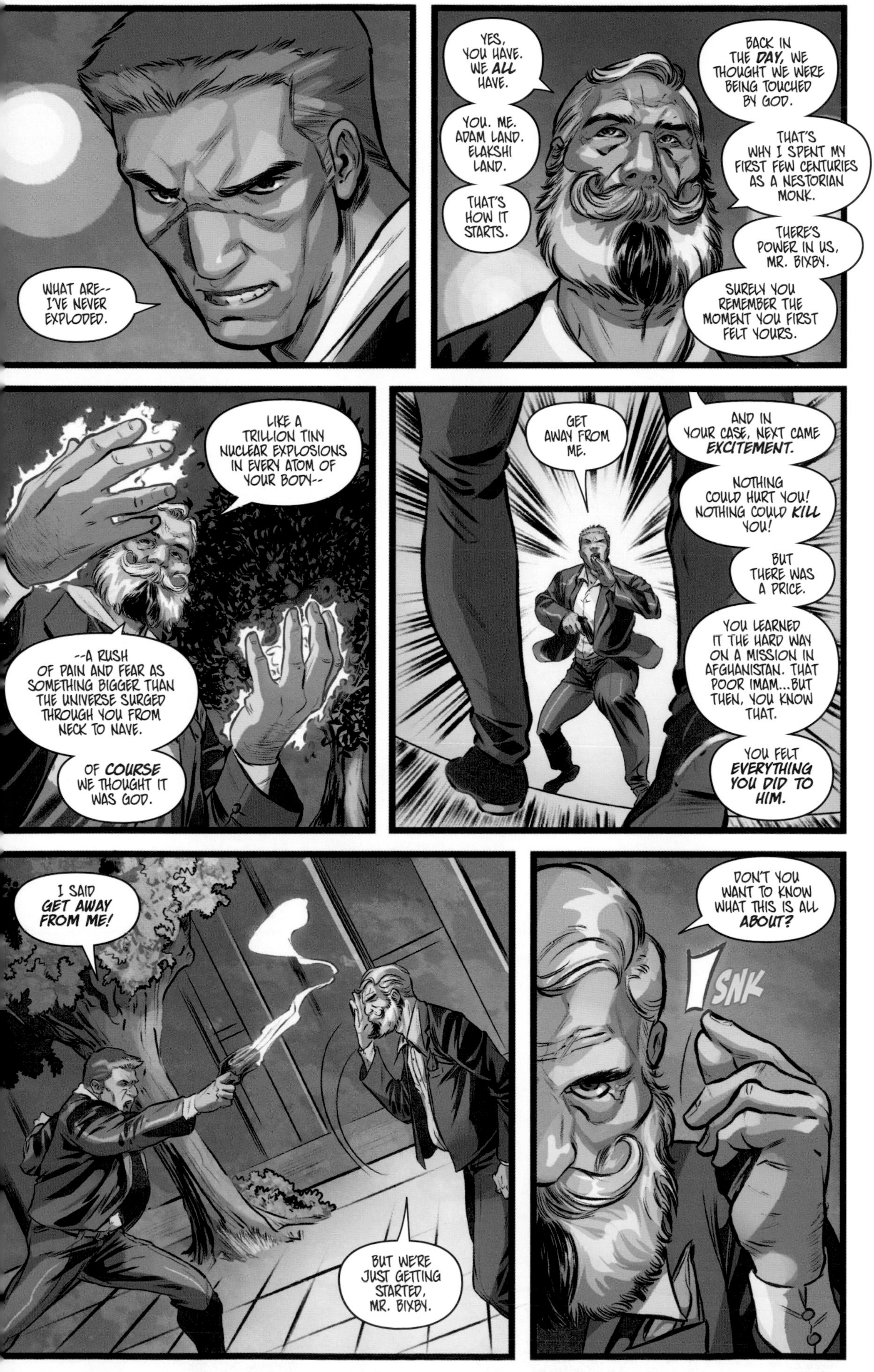
WHAT ARE-- I'VE NEVER EXPLODED.
YES, YOU HAVE. WE ALL HAVE.
YOU. ME. ADAM LAND. ELAKSHI LAND.
THAT'S HOW IT STARTS.
BACK IN THE DAY, WE THOUGHT WE WERE BEING TOUCHED BY GOD.
THAT'S WHY I SPENT MY FIRST FEW CENTURIES AS A NESTORIAN MONK.
THERE'S POWER IN US, MR. BIXBY.
SURELY YOU REMEMBER THE MOMENT YOU FIRST FELT YOURS.
LIKE A TRILLION TINY NUCLEAR EXPLOSIONS IN EVERY ATOM OF YOUR BODY--
--A RUSH OF PAIN AND FEAR AS SOMETHING BIGGER THAN THE UNIVERSE SURGED THROUGH YOU FROM NECK TO NAVE.
OF COURSE WE THOUGHT IT WAS GOD.
GET AWAY FROM ME.
AND IN YOUR CASE, NEXT CAME EXCITEMENT.
NOTHING COULD HURT YOU! NOTHING COULD KILL YOU!
BUT THERE WAS A PRICE.
YOU LEARNED IT THE HARD WAY ON A MISSION IN AFGHANISTAN. THAT POOR IMAM...BUT THEN, YOU KNOW THAT.
YOU FELT EVERYTHING YOU DID TO HIM.
I SAID GET AWAY FROM ME!
BUT WE'RE JUST GETTING STARTED, MR. BIXBY.
DON'T YOU WANT TO KNOW WHAT THIS IS ALL ABOUT?
SNK

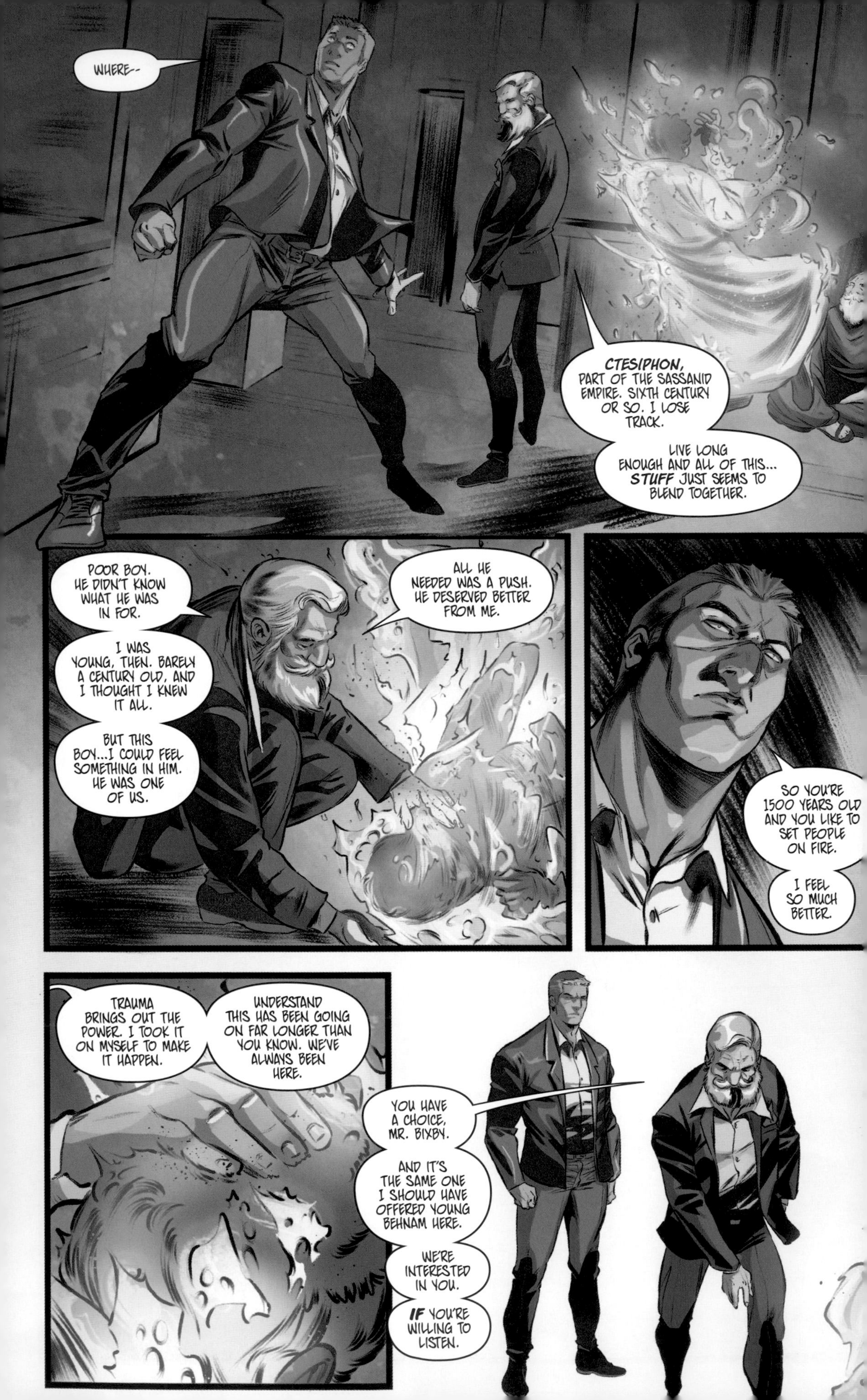
WHERE-
CTESIPHON, PART OF THE SASSANID EMPIRE. SIXTH CENTURY OR SO. I LOSE TRACK.
LIVE LONG ENOUGH AND ALL OF THIS... STUFF JUST SEEMS TO BLEND TOGETHER.
POOR BOY. HE DIDN'T KNOW WHAT HE WAS IN FOR.
I WAS YOUNG, THEN. BARELY A CENTURY OLD, AND I THOUGHT I KNEW IT ALL.
BUT THIS BOY...I COULD FEEL SOMETHING IN HIM. HE WAS ONE OF US.
ALL HE NEEDED WAS A PUSH. HE DESERVED BETTER FROM ME.
SO YOU'RE 1500 YEARS OLD AND YOU LIKE TO SET PEOPLE ON FIRE.
I FEEL SO MUCH BETTER.
TRAUMA BRINGS OUT THE POWER. I TOOK IT ON MYSELF TO MAKE IT HAPPEN.
UNDERSTAND THIS HAS BEEN GOING ON FAR LONGER THAN YOU KNOW. WE'VE ALWAYS BEEN HERE.
YOU HAVE A CHOICE, MR. BIXBY.
AND IT'S THE SAME ONE I SHOULD HAVE OFFERED YOUNG BEHNAM HERE.
WE'RE INTERESTED IN YOU.
IF YOU'RE WILLING TO LISTEN.

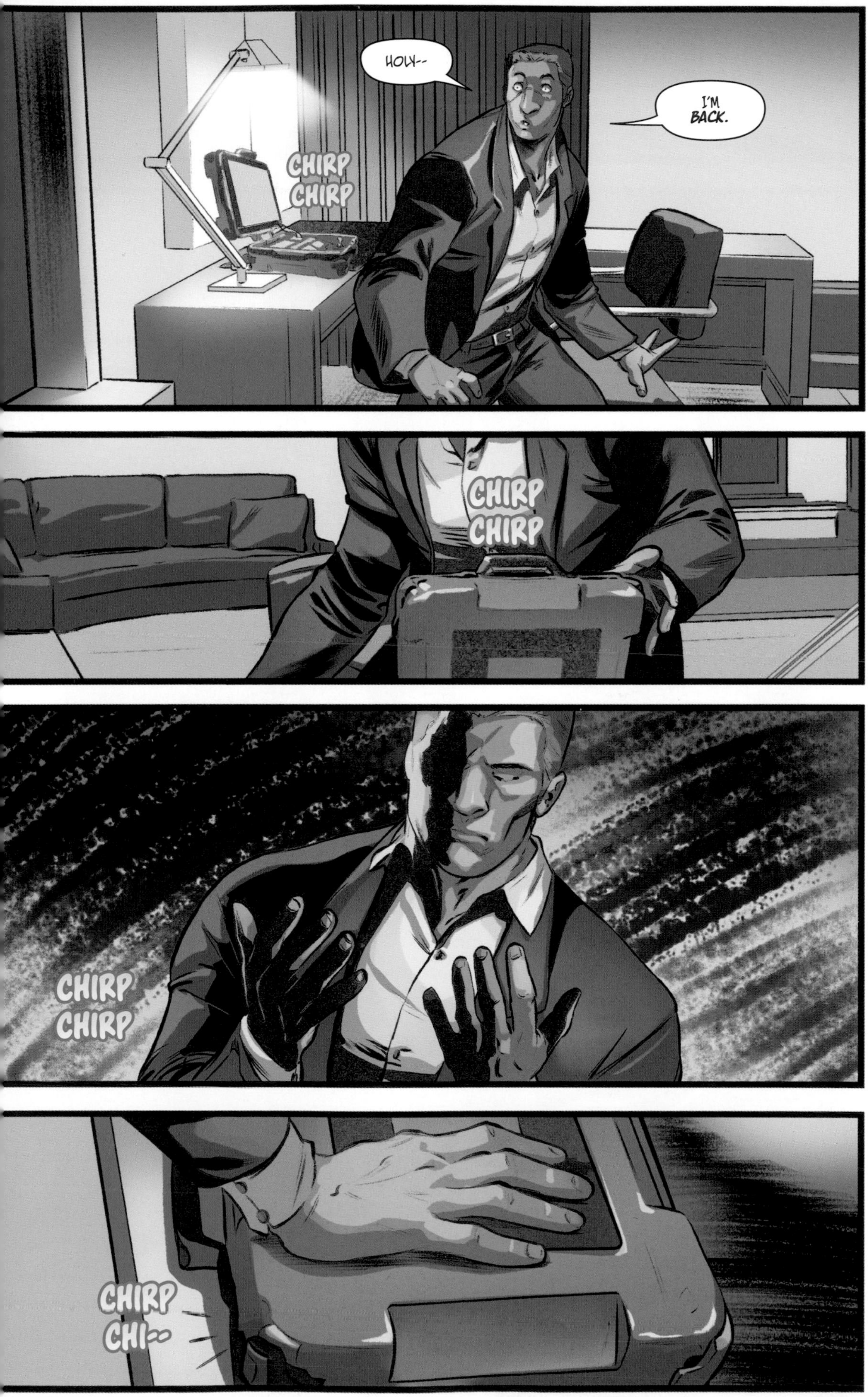
HOLY--
I'M BACK.
CHIRP CHIRP
CHIRP CHIRP
CHIRP CHIRP
CHIRP CHI--

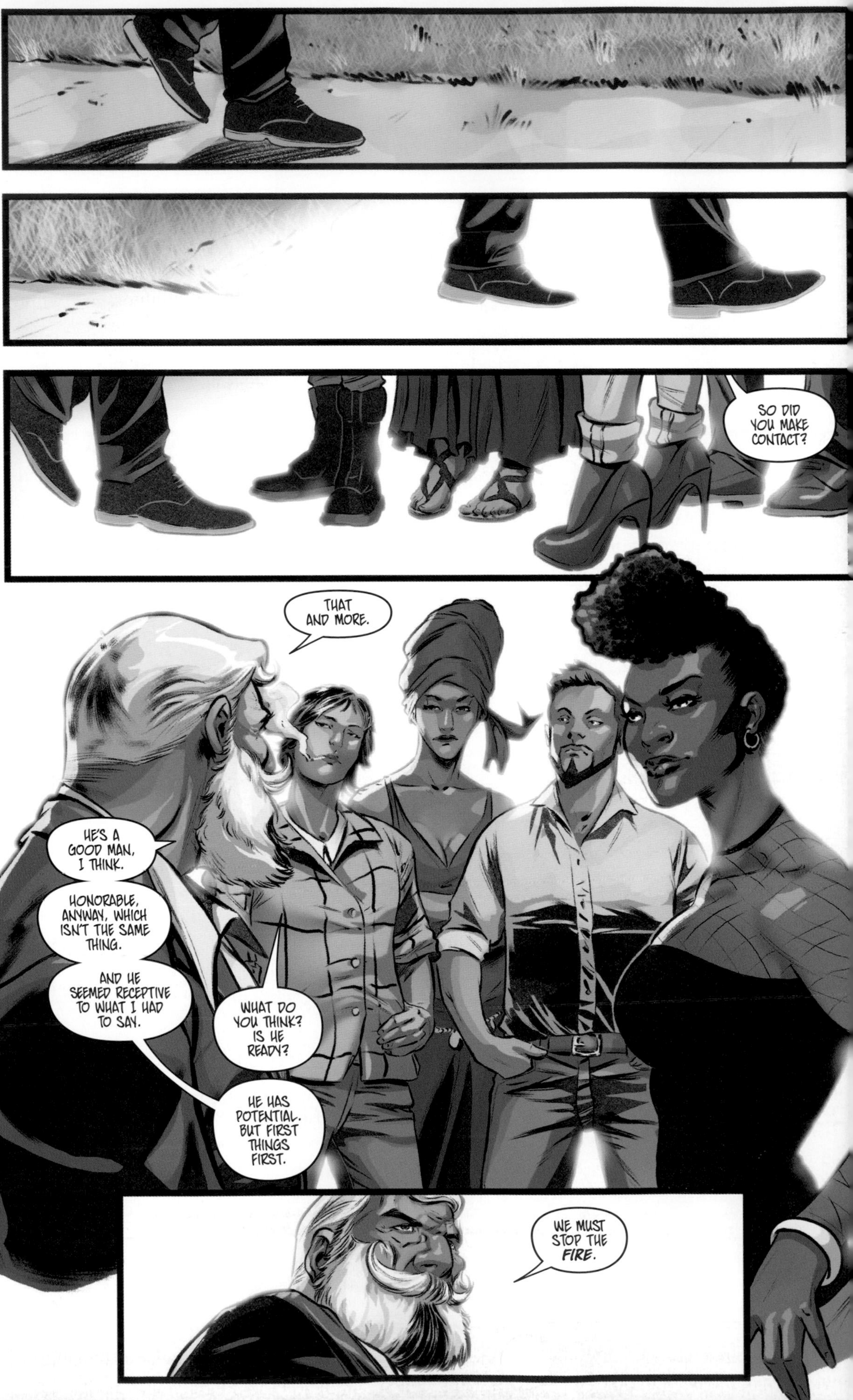
SO DID YOU MAKE CONTACT?
THAT AND MORE.
HE'S A GOOD MAN, I THINK.
HONORABLE, ANYWAY, WHICH ISN'T THE SAME THING.
AND HE SEEMED RECEPTIVE TO WHAT I HAD TO SAY.
WHAT DO YOU THINK? IS HE READY?
HE HAS POTENTIAL. BUT FIRST THINGS FIRST.
WE MUST STOP THE *FIRE*.

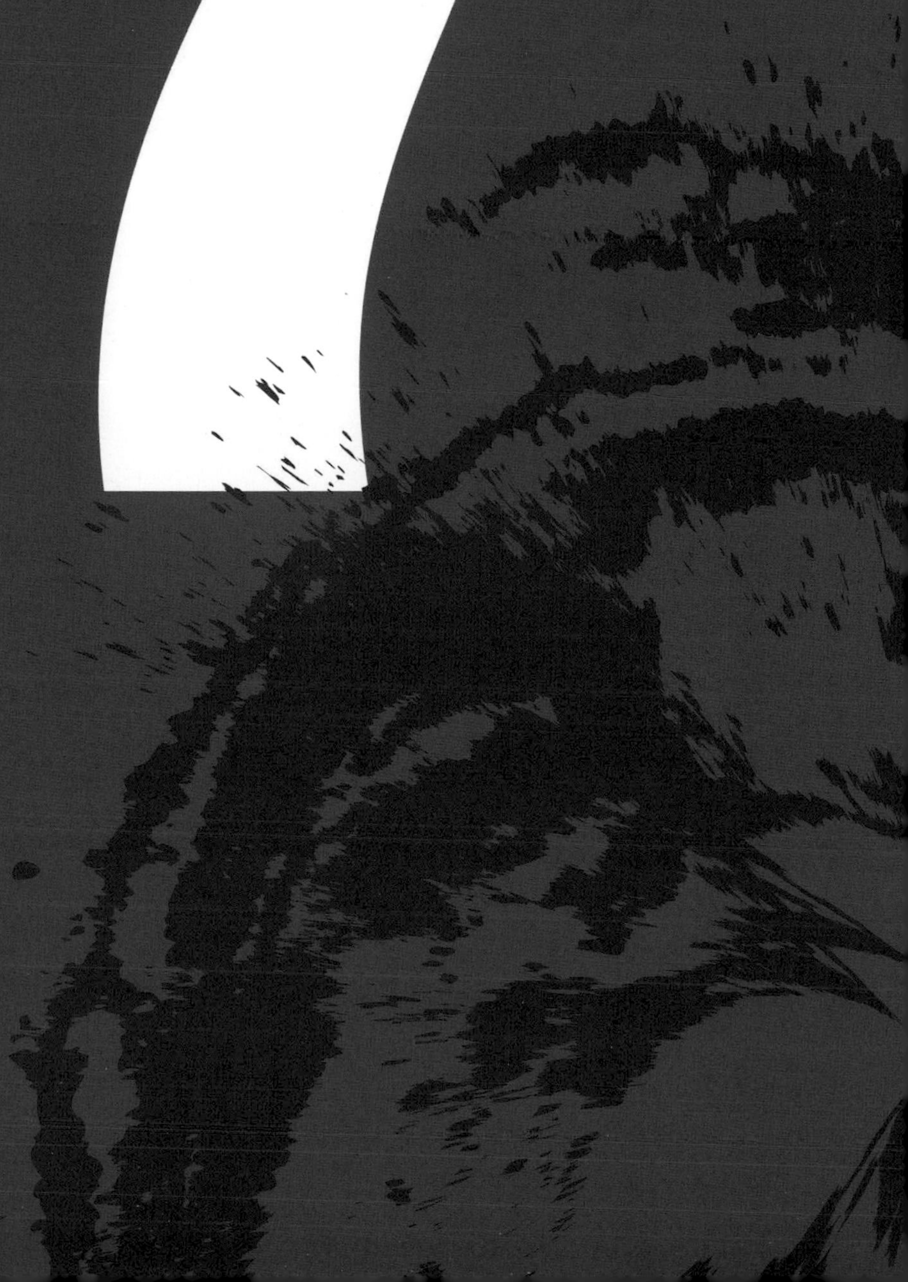

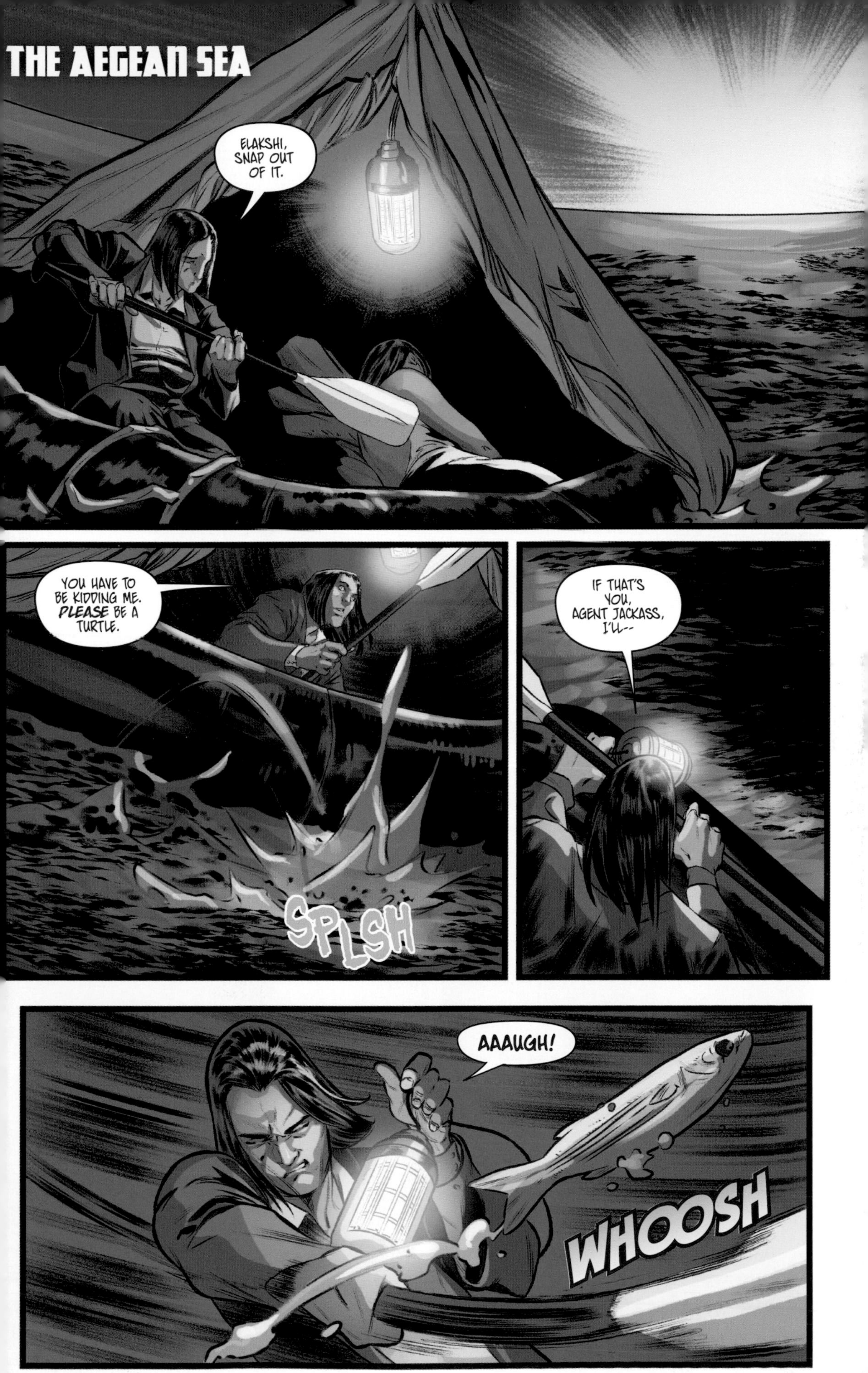
THE AEGEAN SEA
ELAKSHI, SNAP OUT OF IT.
YOU HAVE TO BE KIDDING ME. PLEASE BE A TURTLE.
SPLSH
IF THAT'S YOU, AGENT JACKASS, I'LL--
AAAUGH!
WHOOSH

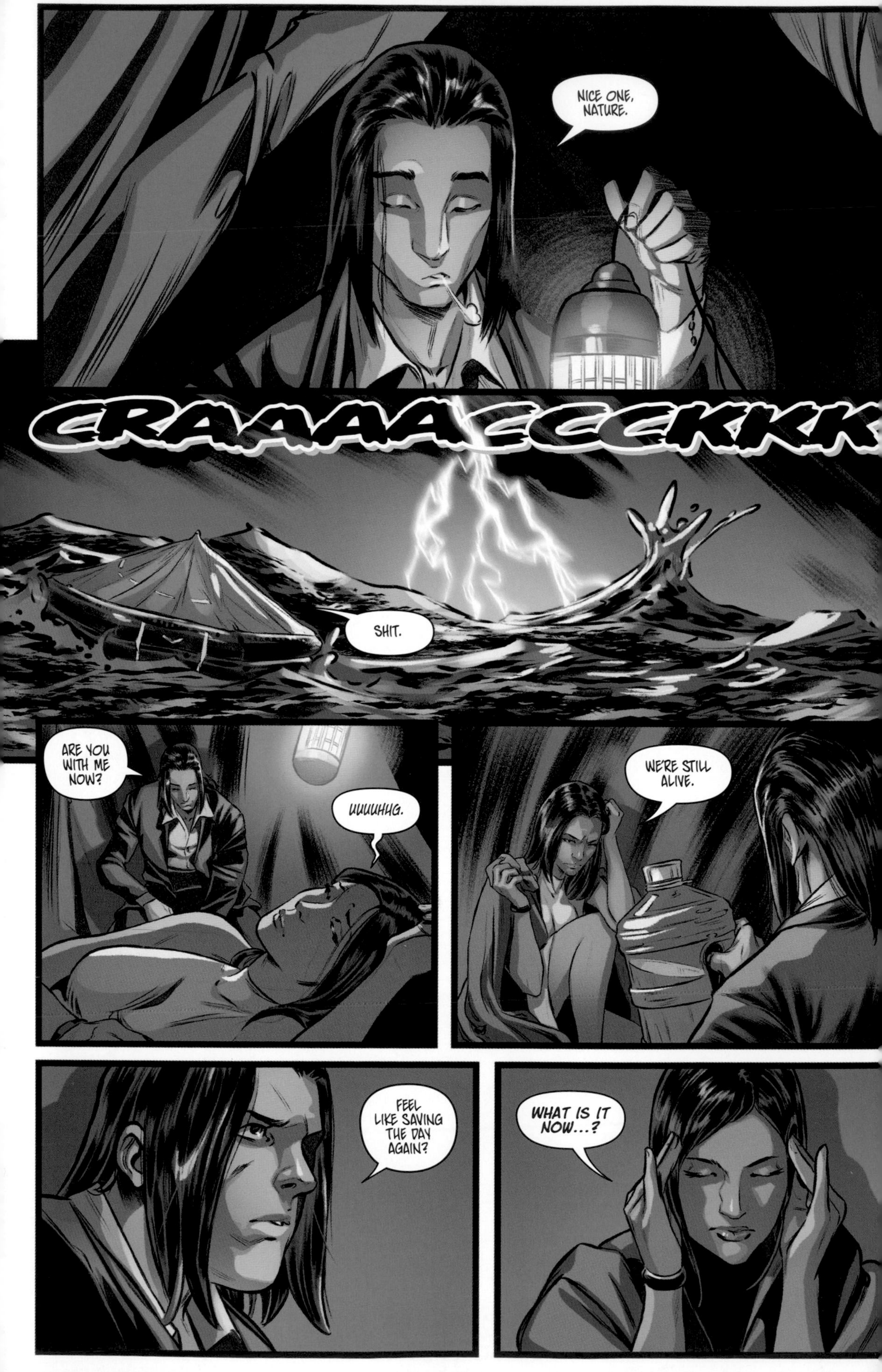
NICE ONE, NATURE.
CRAAAACCCKKK
SHIT.
ARE YOU WITH ME NOW?
UUUUHHG.
WE'RE STILL ALIVE.
FEEL LIKE SAVING THE DAY AGAIN?
WHAT IS IT NOW...?

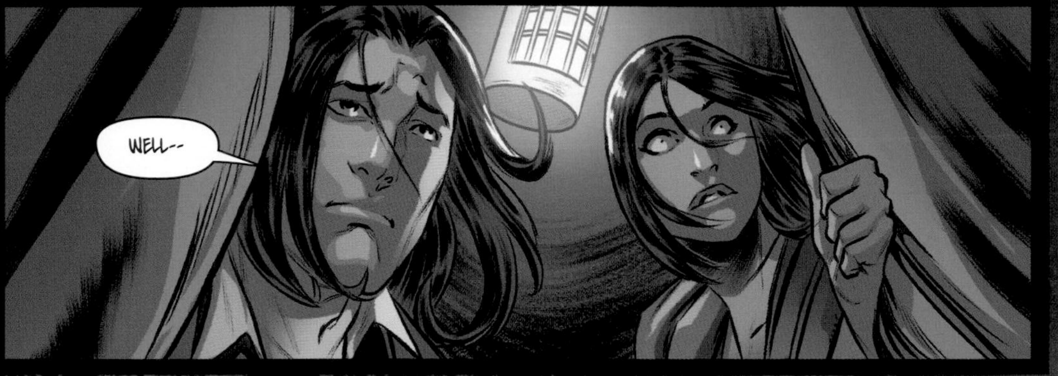
WELL--

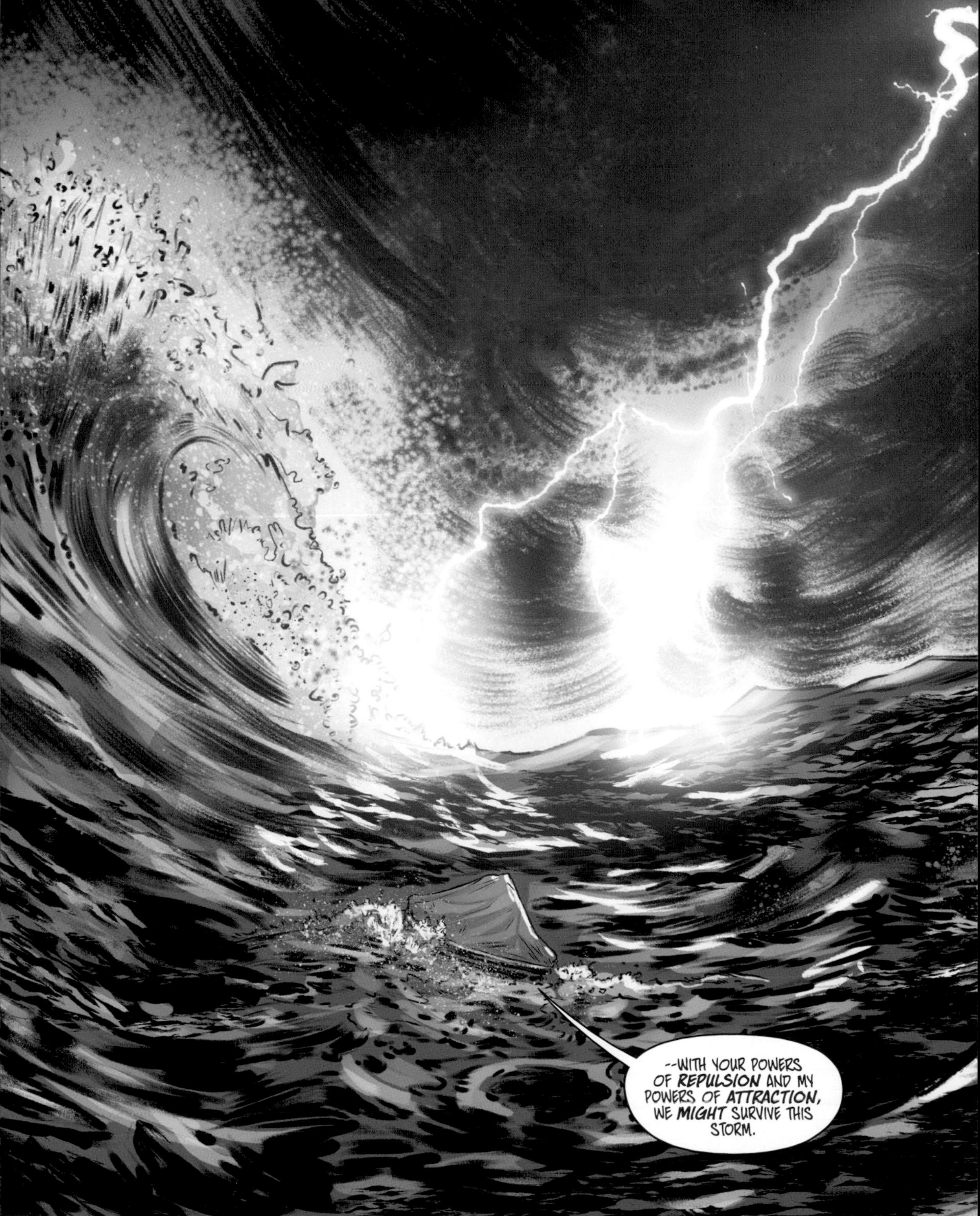
--WITH YOUR POWERS OF REPULSION AND MY POWERS OF ATTRACTION, WE MIGHT SURVIVE THIS STORM.

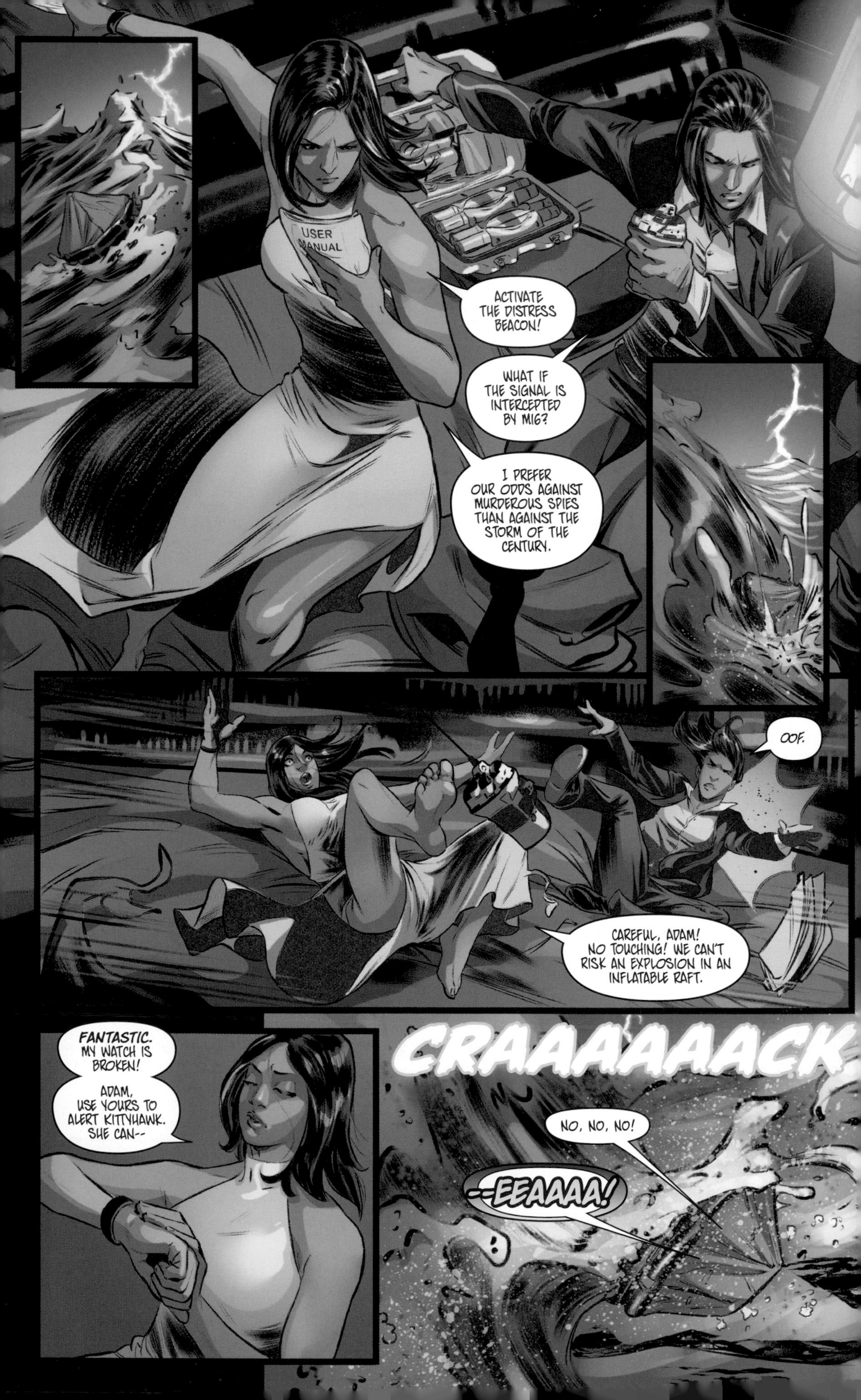
USER MANUAL
ACTIVATE THE DISTRESS BEACON!
WHAT IF THE SIGNAL IS INTERCEPTED BY MI6?
I PREFER OUR ODDS AGAINST MURDEROUS SPIES THAN AGAINST THE STORM OF THE CENTURY.
OOF.
CAREFUL, ADAM! NO TOUCHING! WE CAN'T RISK AN EXPLOSION IN AN INFLATABLE RAFT.
FANTASTIC. MY WATCH IS BROKEN!
ADAM, USE YOURS TO ALERT KITTYHAWK. SHE CAN--
CRAAAAAACK
NO, NO, NO!
--EEAAAA!

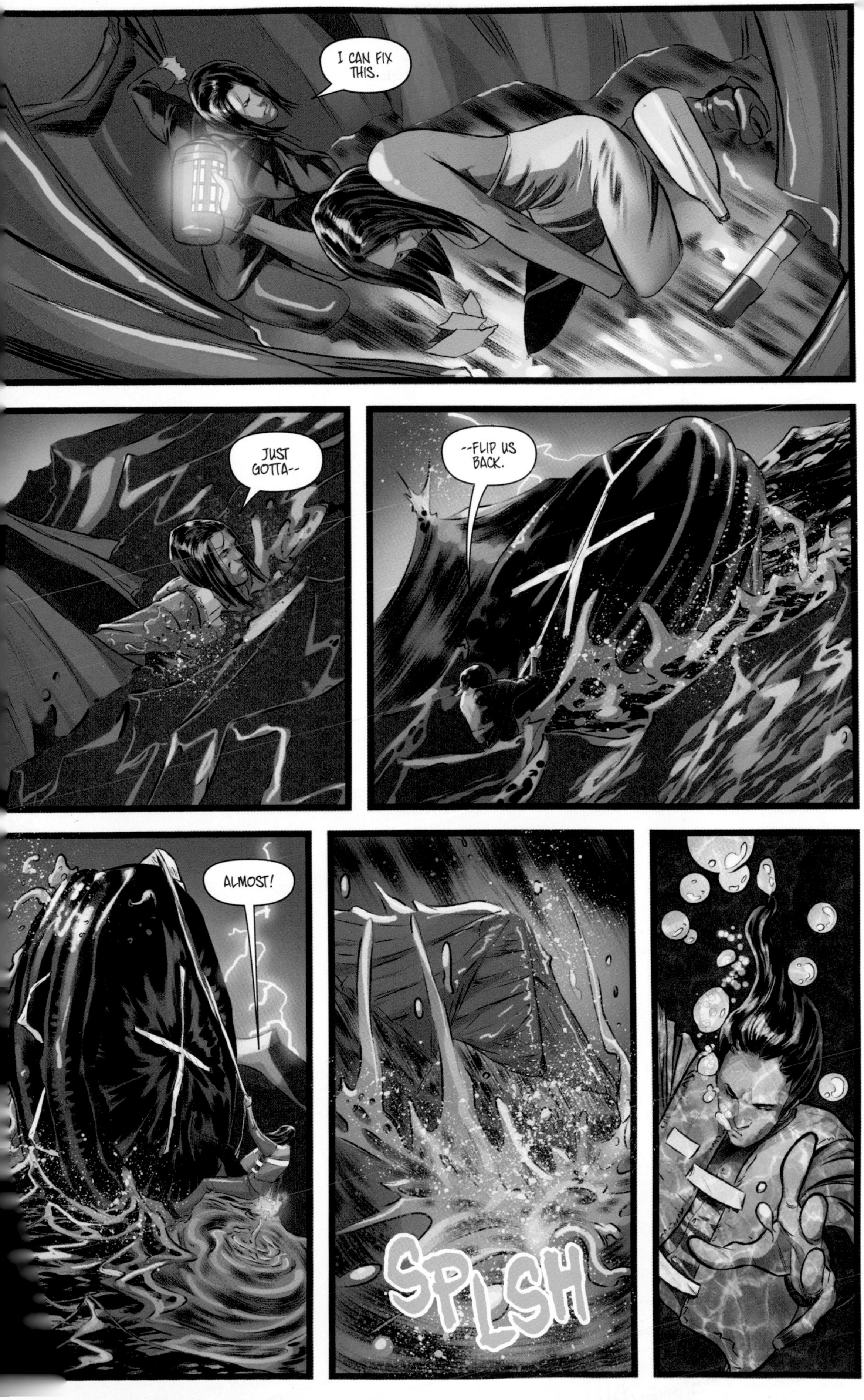
I CAN FIX THIS.
JUST GOTTA--
--FLIP US BACK.
ALMOST!
SPLSH

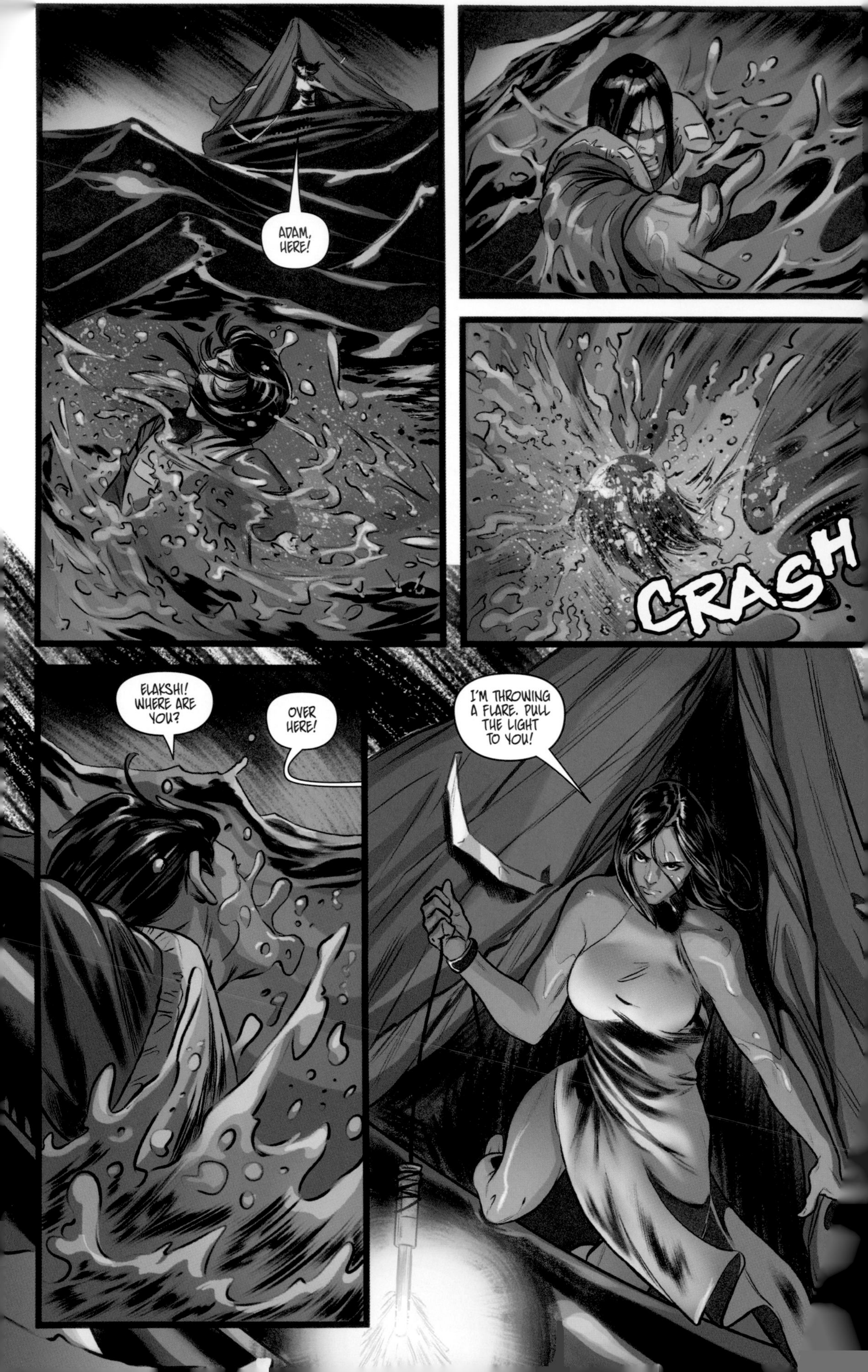
ADAM, HERE!
CRASH
ELAKSHI! WHERE ARE YOU?
OVER HERE!
I'M THROWING A FLARE. PULL THE LIGHT TO YOU!

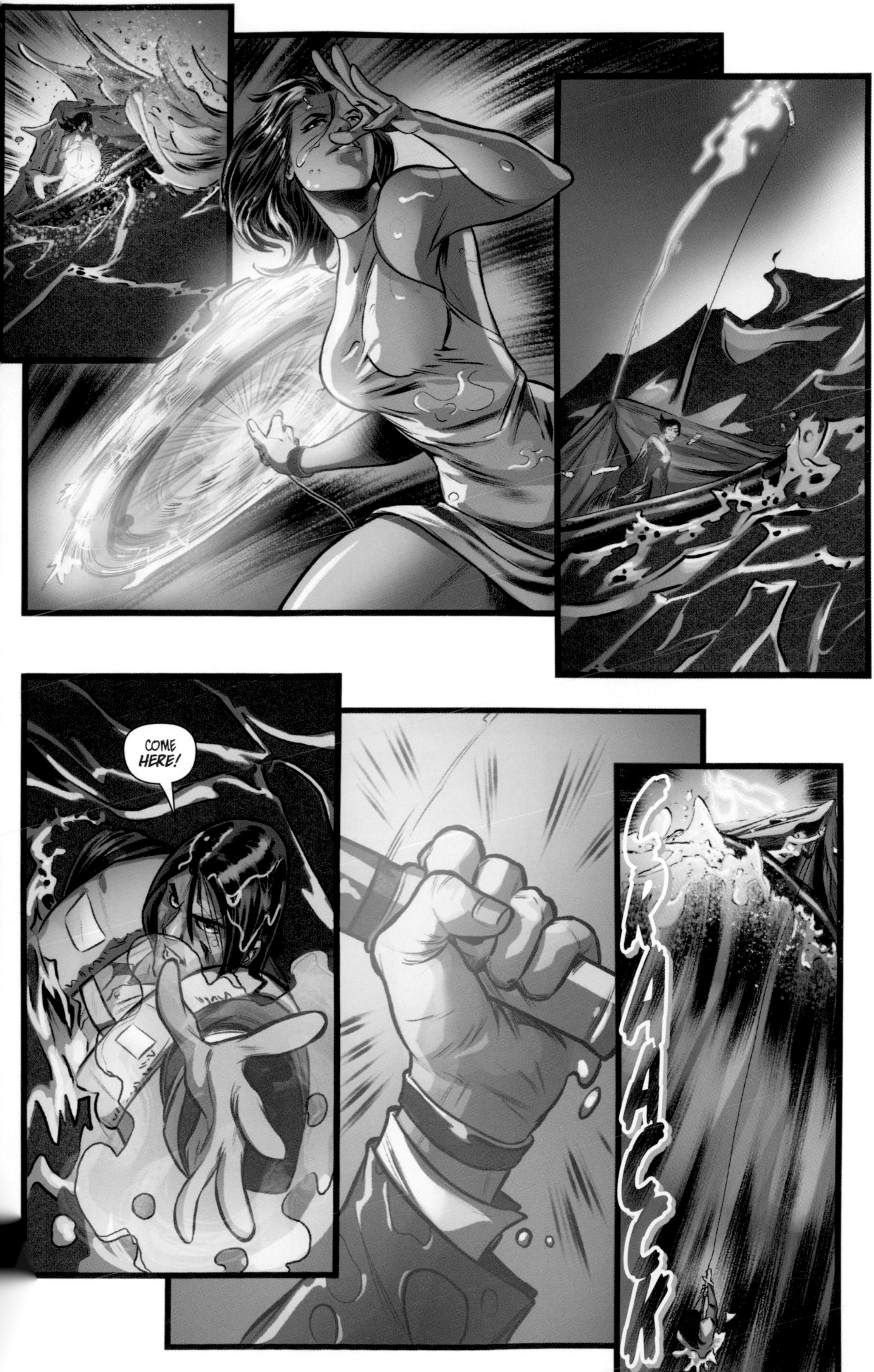
COME HERE!
CRAAACK

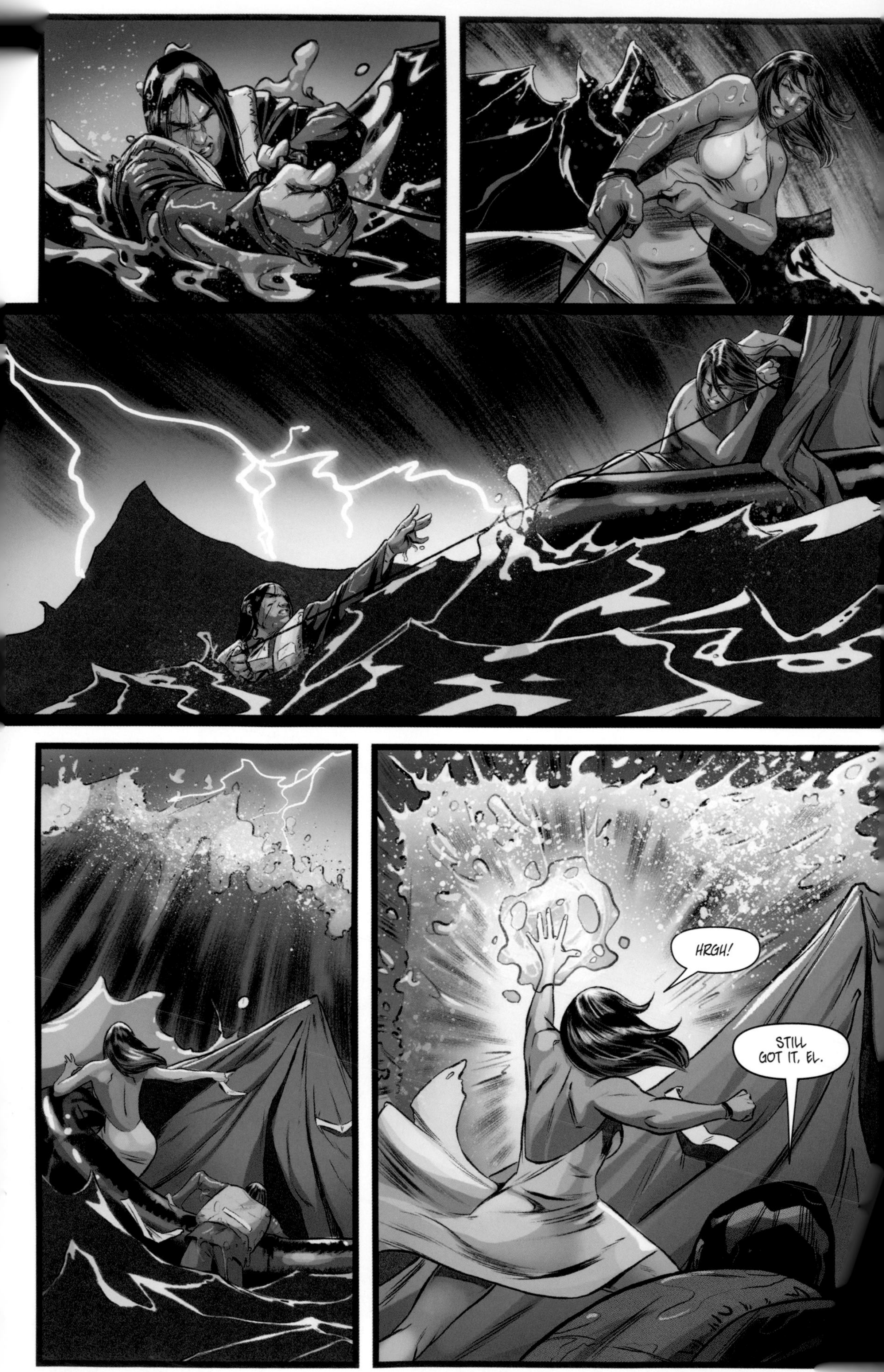
HRGH!
STILL GOT IT, EL.

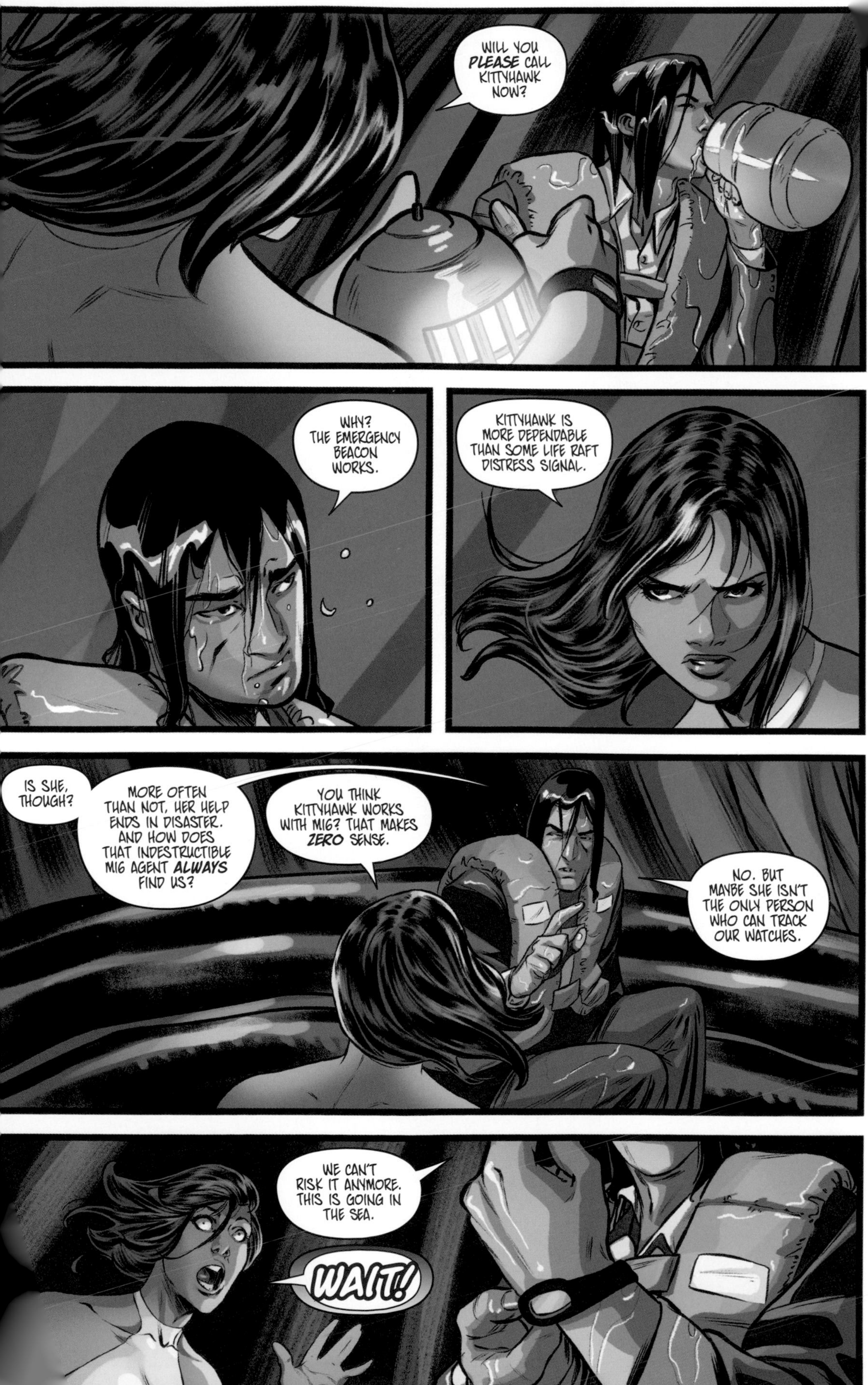
WILL YOU PLEASE CALL KITTYHAWK NOW?
WHY? THE EMERGENCY BEACON WORKS.
KITTYHAWK IS MORE DEPENDABLE THAN SOME LIFE RAFT DISTRESS SIGNAL.
IS SHE, THOUGH?
MORE OFTEN THAN NOT, HER HELP ENDS IN DISASTER. AND HOW DOES THAT INDESTRUCTIBLE MI6 AGENT ALWAYS FIND US?
YOU THINK KITTYHAWK WORKS WITH MI6? THAT MAKES ZERO SENSE.
NO. BUT MAYBE SHE ISN'T THE ONLY PERSON WHO CAN TRACK OUR WATCHES.
WE CAN'T RISK IT ANYMORE. THIS IS GOING IN THE SEA.
WAIT!

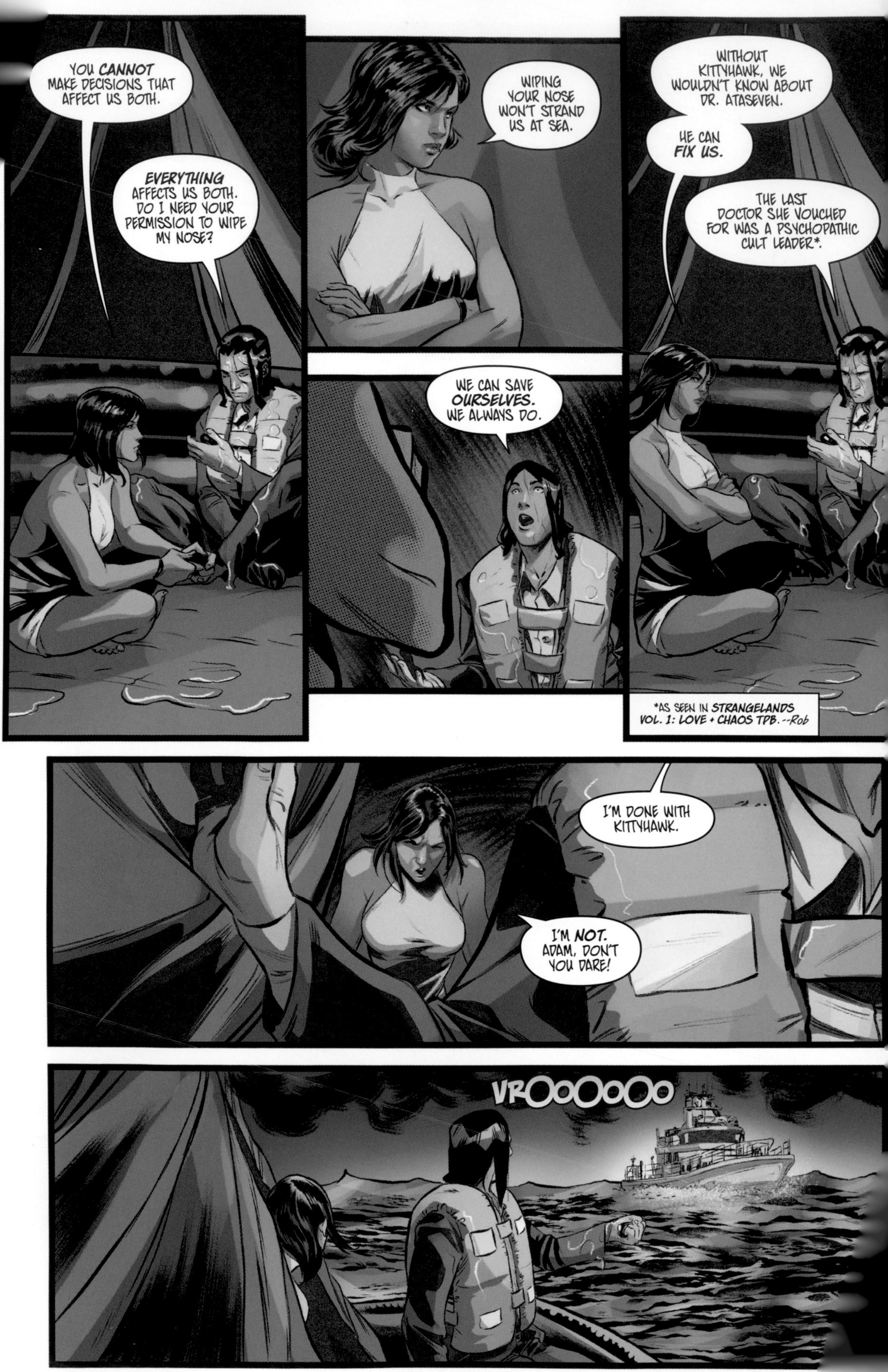
YOU CANNOT MAKE DECISIONS THAT AFFECT US BOTH.
EVERYTHING AFFECTS US BOTH. DO I NEED YOUR PERMISSION TO WIPE MY NOSE?
WIPING YOUR NOSE WON'T STRAND US AT SEA.
WE CAN SAVE OURSELVES. WE ALWAYS DO.
WITHOUT KITTYHAWK, WE WOULDN'T KNOW ABOUT DR. ATASEVEN.
HE CAN FIX US.
THE LAST DOCTOR SHE VOUCHED FOR WAS A PSYCHOPATHIC CULT LEADER*.
*AS SEEN IN STRANGELANDS VOL. 1: LOVE + CHAOS TPB. --Rob
I'M DONE WITH KITTYHAWK.
I'M NOT. ADAM, DON'T YOU DARE!
VROOOOOOO

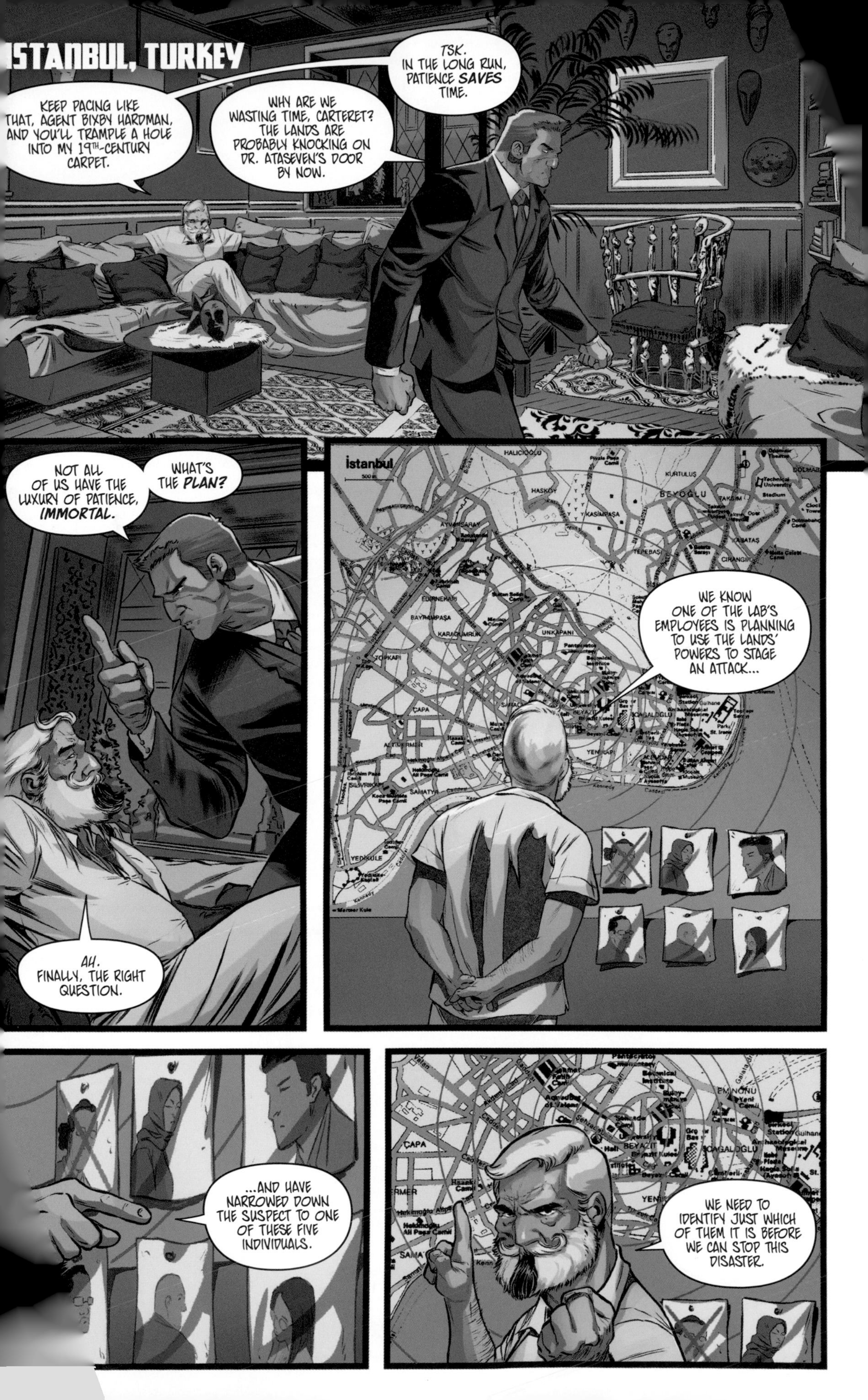
ISTANBUL, TURKEY
KEEP PACING LIKE THAT, AGENT BIXBY HARDMAN, AND YOU'LL TRAMPLE A HOLE INTO MY 19TH-CENTURY CARPET.
WHY ARE WE WASTING TIME, CARTERET? THE LANDS ARE PROBABLY KNOCKING ON DR. ATASEVEN'S DOOR BY NOW.
TSK. IN THE LONG RUN, PATIENCE SAVES TIME.
NOT ALL OF US HAVE THE LUXURY OF PATIENCE, IMMORTAL.
WHAT'S THE PLAN?
AH. FINALLY, THE RIGHT QUESTION.
İstanbul
WE KNOW ONE OF THE LAB'S EMPLOYEES IS PLANNING TO USE THE LANDS' POWERS TO STAGE AN ATTACK...
...AND HAVE NARROWED DOWN THE SUSPECT TO ONE OF THESE FIVE INDIVIDUALS.
WE NEED TO IDENTIFY JUST WHICH OF THEM IT IS BEFORE WE CAN STOP THIS DISASTER.

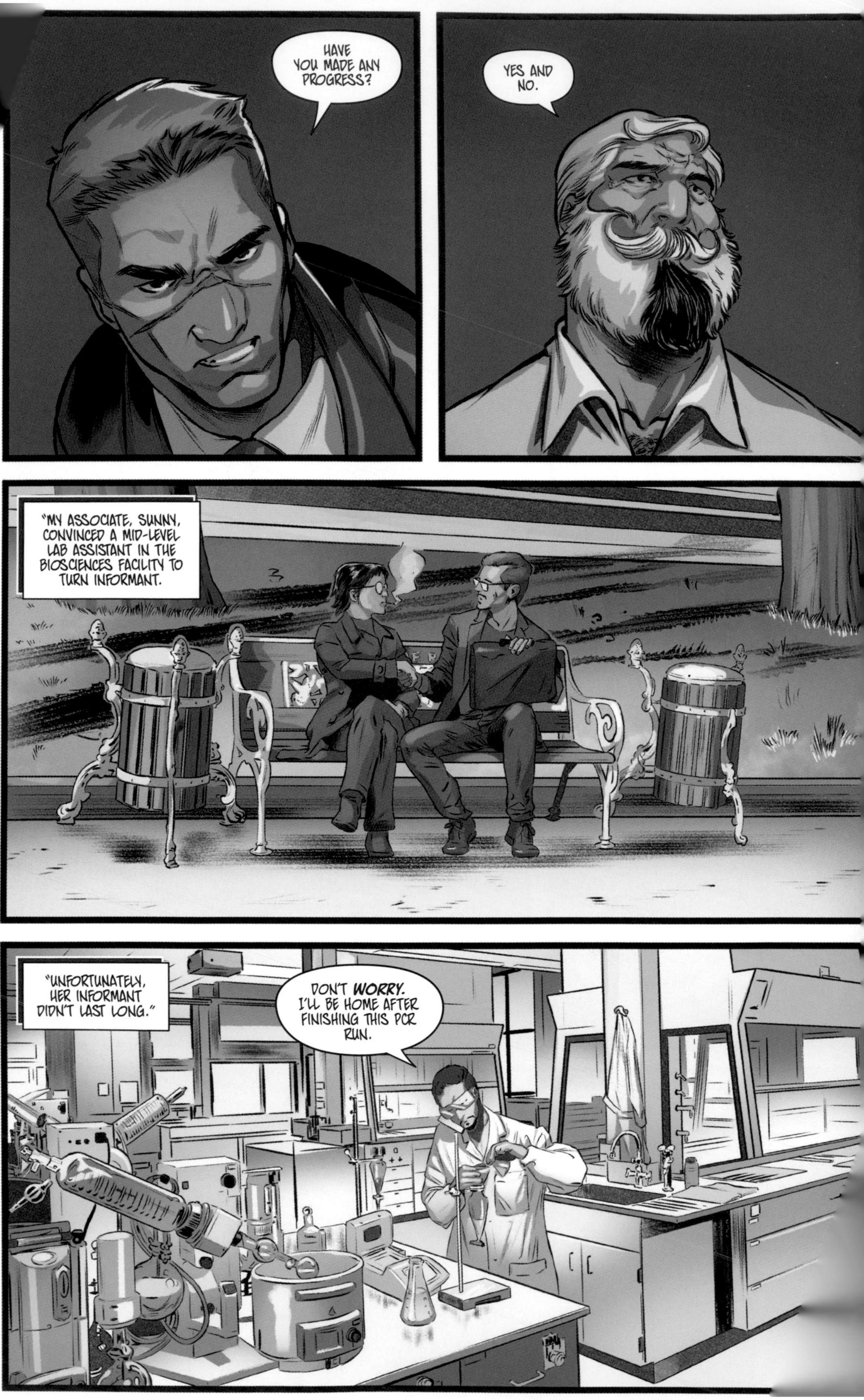
HAVE YOU MADE ANY PROGRESS?
YES AND NO.
"MY ASSOCIATE, SUNNY, CONVINCED A MID-LEVEL LAB ASSISTANT IN THE BIOSCIENCES FACILITY TO TURN INFORMANT.
"UNFORTUNATELY, HER INFORMANT DIDN'T LAST LONG."
DON'T **WORRY.** I'LL BE HOME AFTER FINISHING THIS PCR RUN.

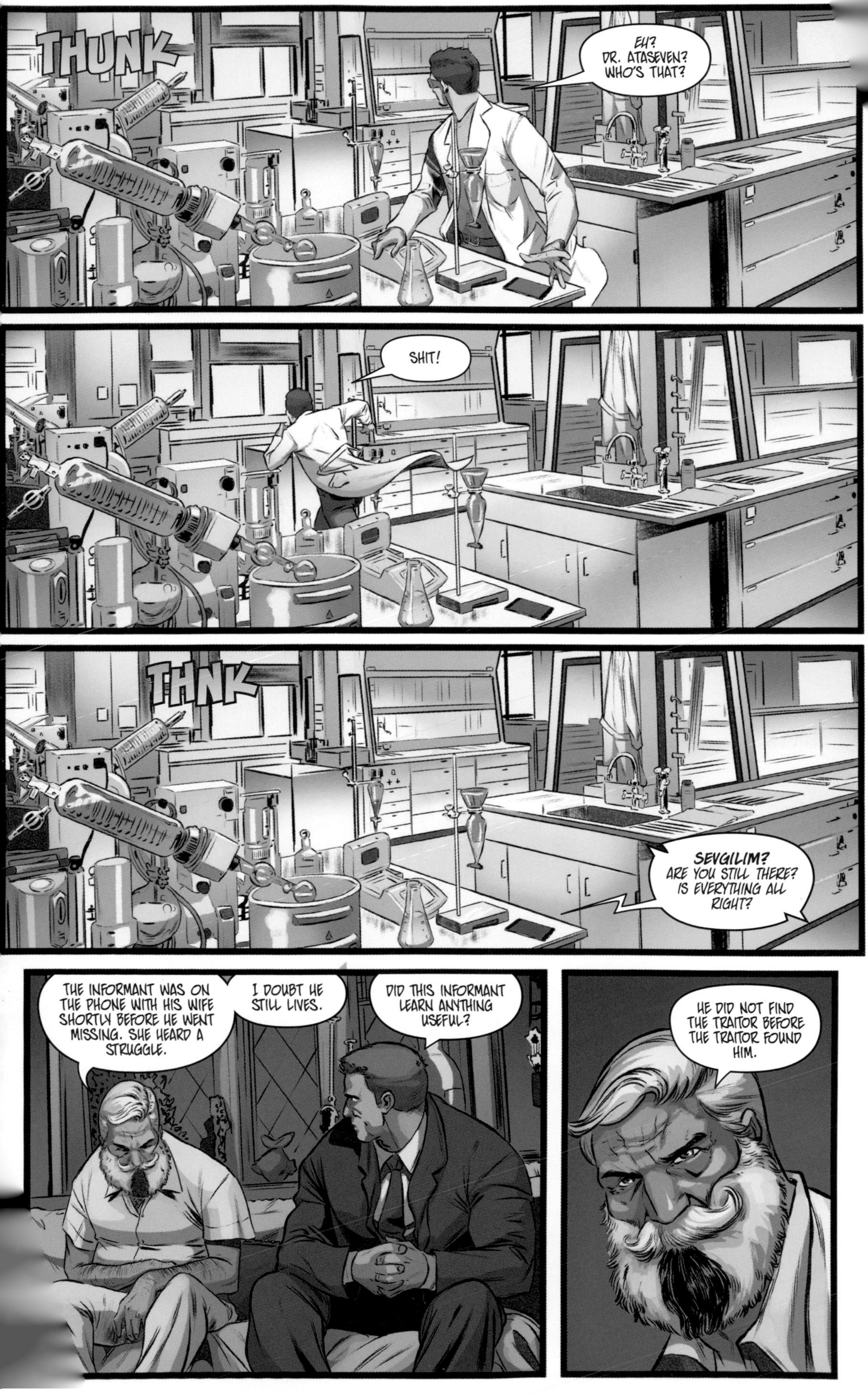
THUNK
EH?
DR. ATASEVEN?
WHO'S THAT?
SHIT!
THNK
SEVGILIM?
ARE YOU STILL THERE?
IS EVERYTHING ALL
RIGHT?
THE INFORMANT WAS ON THE PHONE WITH HIS WIFE SHORTLY BEFORE HE WENT MISSING. SHE HEARD A STRUGGLE.
I DOUBT HE STILL LIVES.
DID THIS INFORMANT LEARN ANYTHING USEFUL?
HE DID NOT FIND THE TRAITOR BEFORE THE TRAITOR FOUND HIM.

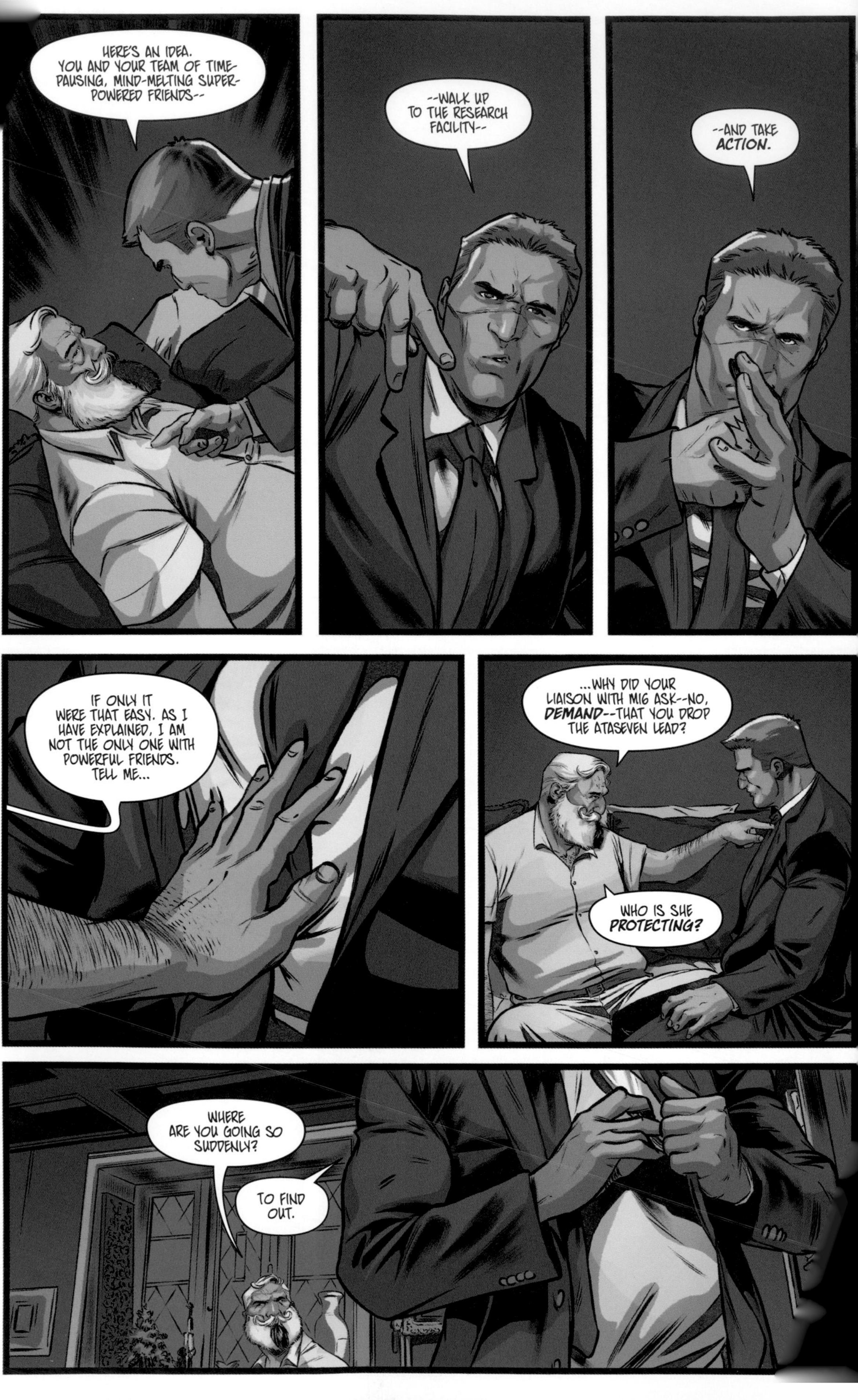
HERE'S AN IDEA. YOU AND YOUR TEAM OF TIME-PAUSING, MIND-MELTING SUPER-POWERED FRIENDS--
--WALK UP TO THE RESEARCH FACILITY--
--AND TAKE ACTION.
IF ONLY IT WERE THAT EASY. AS I HAVE EXPLAINED, I AM NOT THE ONLY ONE WITH POWERFUL FRIENDS. TELL ME...
...WHY DID YOUR LIAISON WITH MIG ASK--NO, DEMAND--THAT YOU DROP THE ATASEVEN LEAD?
WHO IS SHE PROTECTING?
WHERE ARE YOU GOING SO SUDDENLY?
TO FIND OUT.

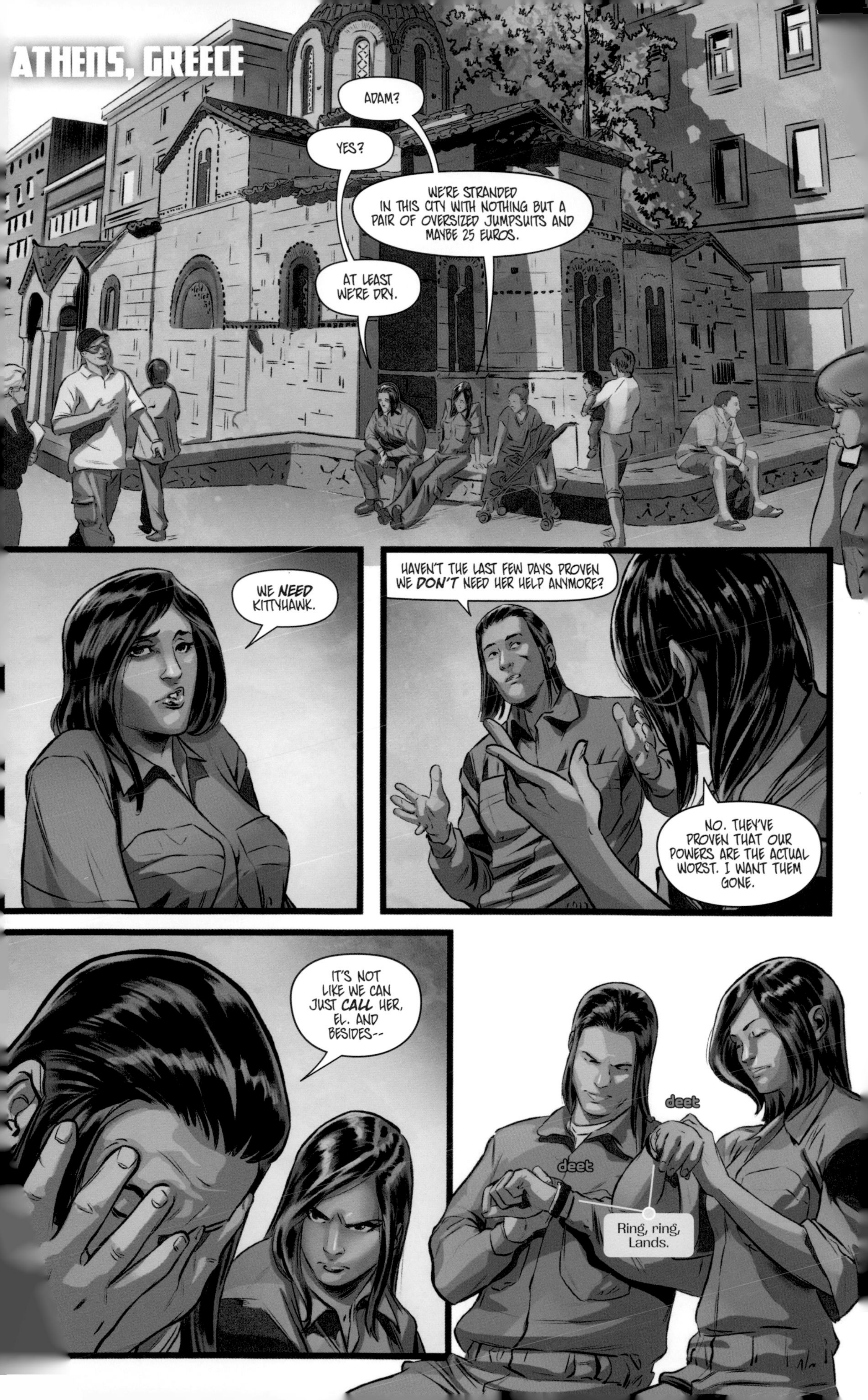
ATHENS, GREECE
ADAM?
YES?
WE'RE STRANDED IN THIS CITY WITH NOTHING BUT A PAIR OF OVERSIZED JUMPSUITS AND MAYBE 25 EUROS.
AT LEAST WE'RE DRY.
WE NEED KITTYHAWK.
HAVEN'T THE LAST FEW DAYS PROVEN WE DON'T NEED HER HELP ANYMORE?
NO. THEY'VE PROVEN THAT OUR POWERS ARE THE ACTUAL WORST. I WANT THEM GONE.
IT'S NOT LIKE WE CAN JUST CALL HER, EL. AND BESIDES--
deet
deet
Ring, ring, Lands.

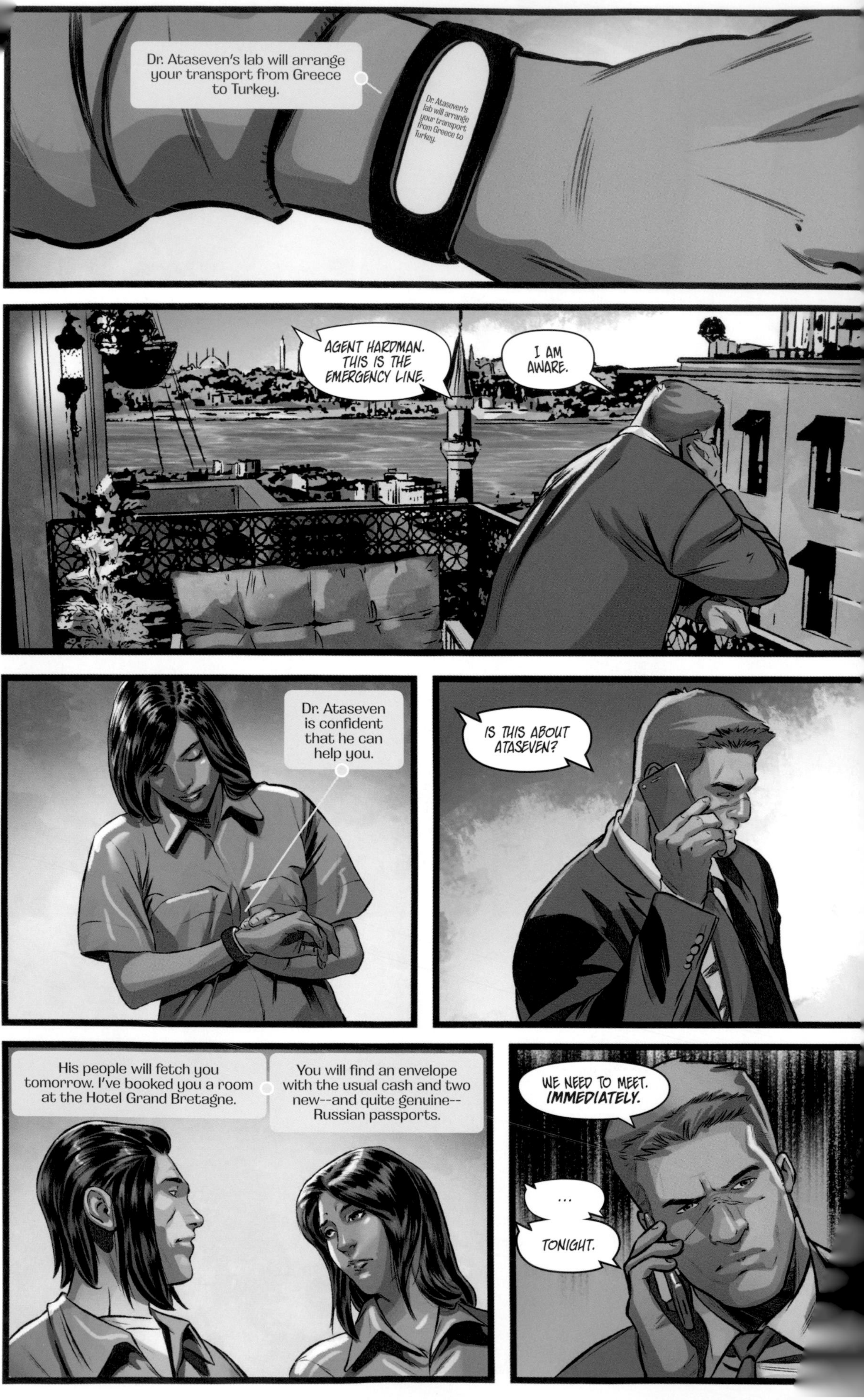
Dr. Ataseven's lab will arrange your transport from Greece to Turkey.
Dr. Ataseven's lab will arrange your transport from Greece to Turkey.
AGENT HARDMAN. THIS IS THE EMERGENCY LINE.
I AM AWARE.
Dr. Ataseven is confident that he can help you.
IS THIS ABOUT ATASEVEN?
His people will fetch you tomorrow. I've booked you a room at the Hotel Grand Bretagne.
You will find an envelope with the usual cash and two new--and quite genuine--Russian passports.
WE NEED TO MEET. *IMMEDIATELY.*
...
TONIGHT.

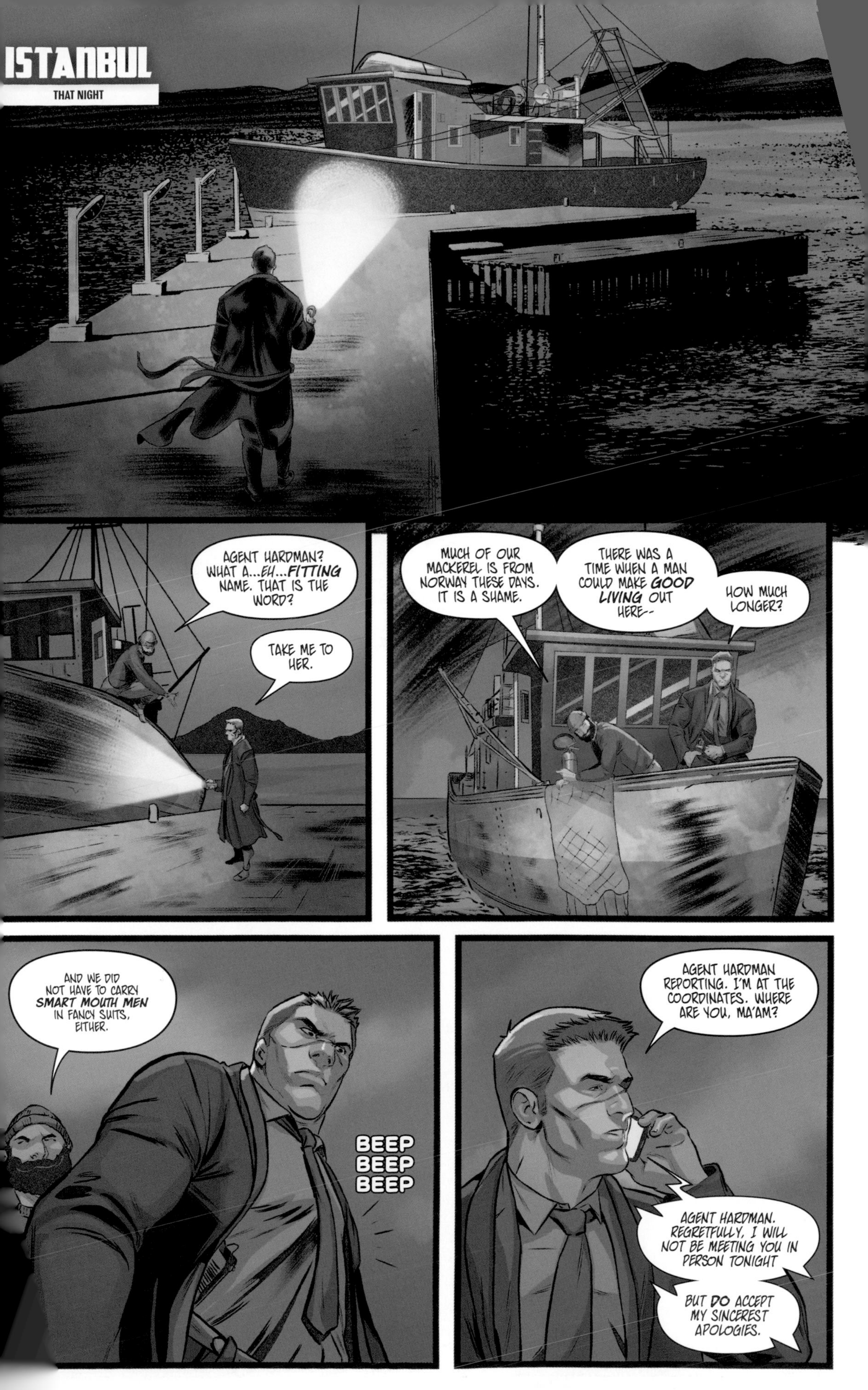
ISTANBUL
THAT NIGHT
AGENT HARDMAN? WHAT A...EH...FITTING NAME. THAT IS THE WORD?
TAKE ME TO HER.
MUCH OF OUR MACKEREL IS FROM NORWAY THESE DAYS. IT IS A SHAME.
THERE WAS A TIME WHEN A MAN COULD MAKE GOOD LIVING OUT HERE--
HOW MUCH LONGER?
AND WE DID NOT HAVE TO CARRY SMART MOUTH MEN IN FANCY SUITS, EITHER.
BEEP BEEP BEEP
AGENT HARDMAN REPORTING. I'M AT THE COORDINATES. WHERE ARE YOU, MA'AM?
AGENT HARDMAN. REGRETFULLY, I WILL NOT BE MEETING YOU IN PERSON TONIGHT
BUT DO ACCEPT MY SINCEREST APOLOGIES.

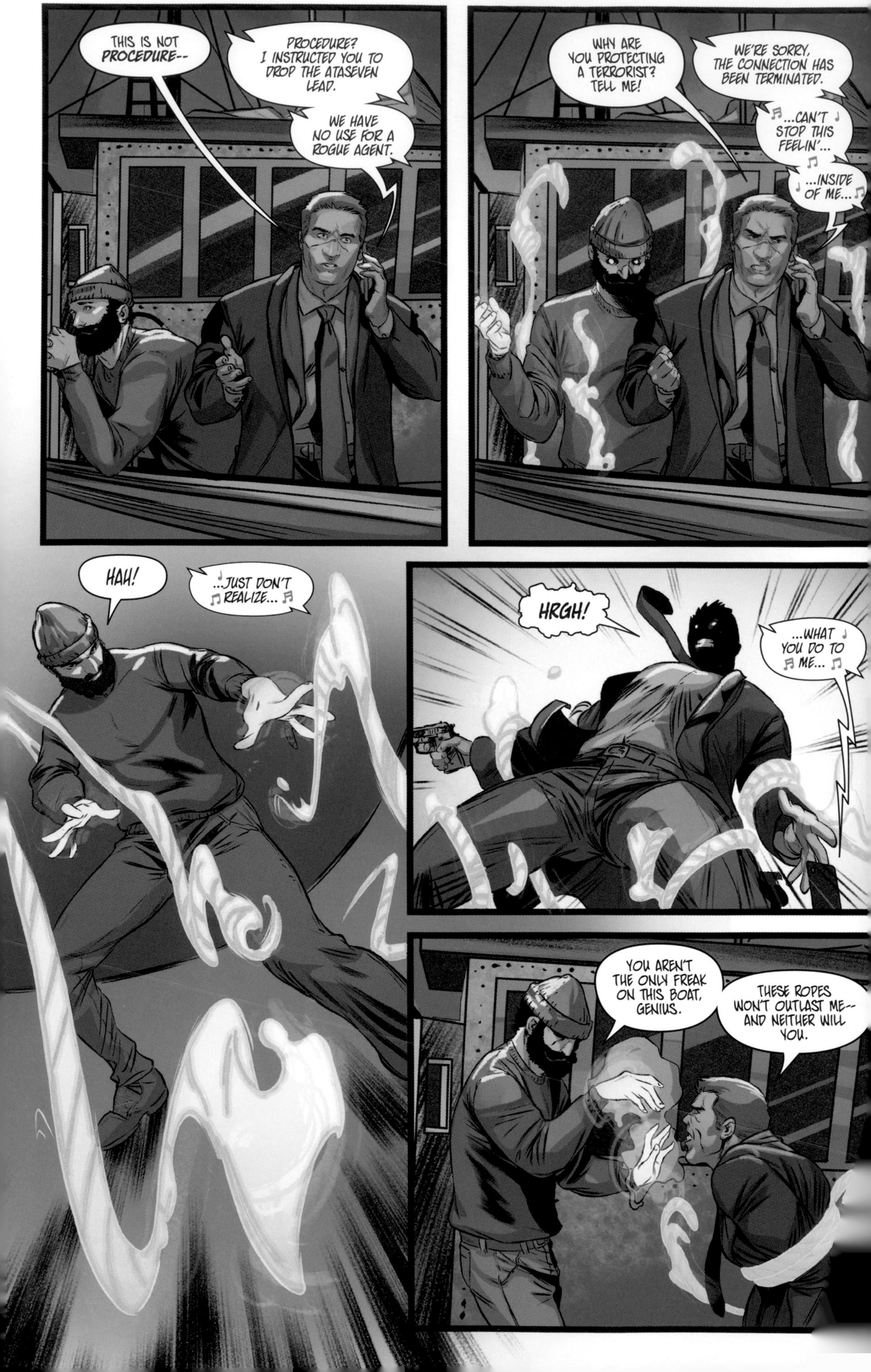
THIS IS NOT PROCEDURE--
PROCEDURE? I INSTRUCTED YOU TO DROP THE ATASEVEN LEAD.
WE HAVE NO USE FOR A ROGUE AGENT.
WHY ARE YOU PROTECTING A TERRORIST? TELL ME!
WE'RE SORRY, THE CONNECTION HAS BEEN TERMINATED.
...CAN'T STOP THIS FEELIN'...
...INSIDE OF ME...
HAH!
...JUST DON'T REALIZE...
HRGH!
...WHAT YOU DO TO ME...
YOU AREN'T THE ONLY FREAK ON THIS BOAT, GENIUS.
THESE ROPES WON'T OUTLAST ME-- AND NEITHER WILL YOU.

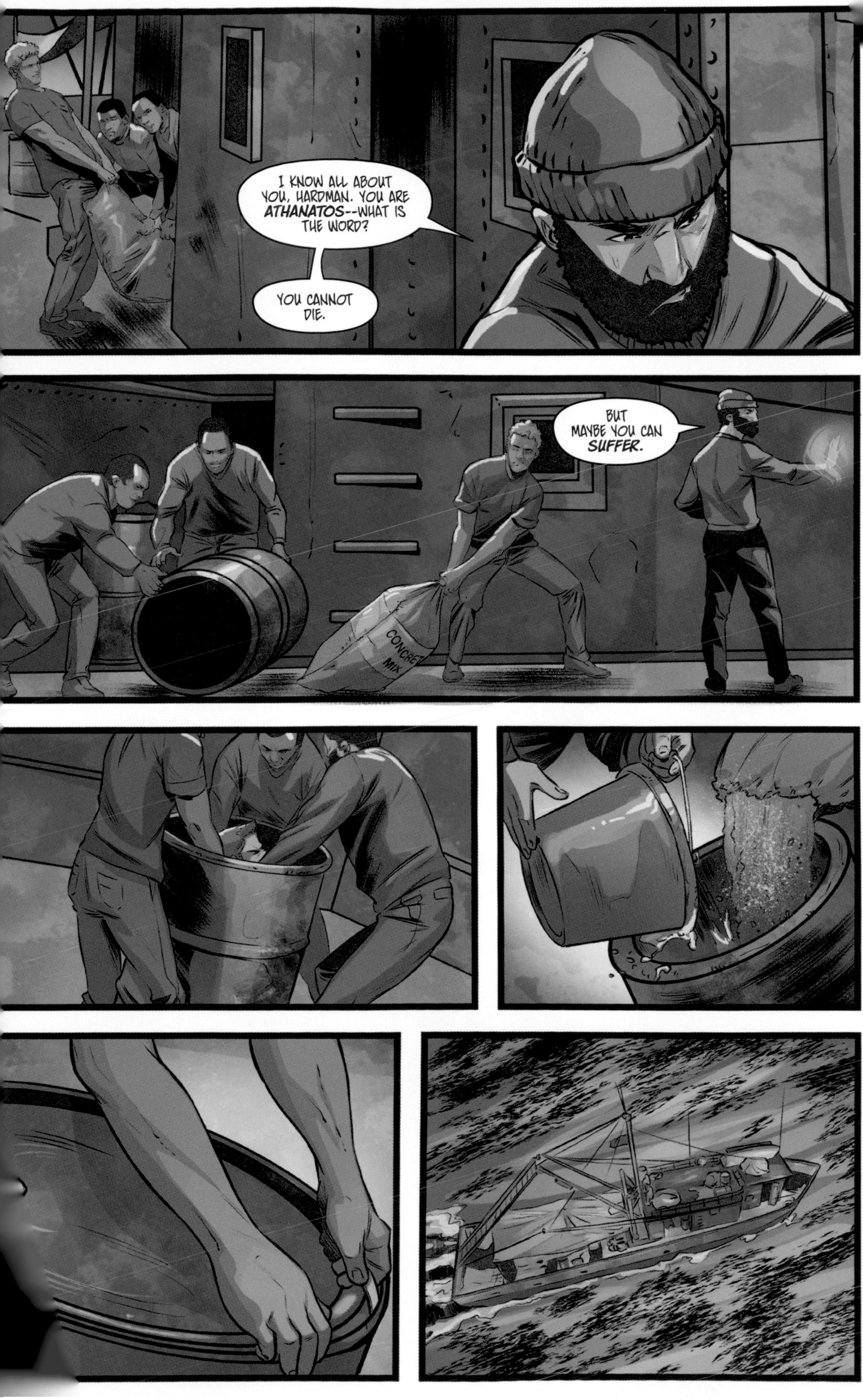

I KNOW ALL ABOUT YOU, HARDMAN. YOU ARE **ATHANATOS**--WHAT IS THE WORD?
YOU CANNOT DIE.
BUT MAYBE YOU CAN **SUFFER**.

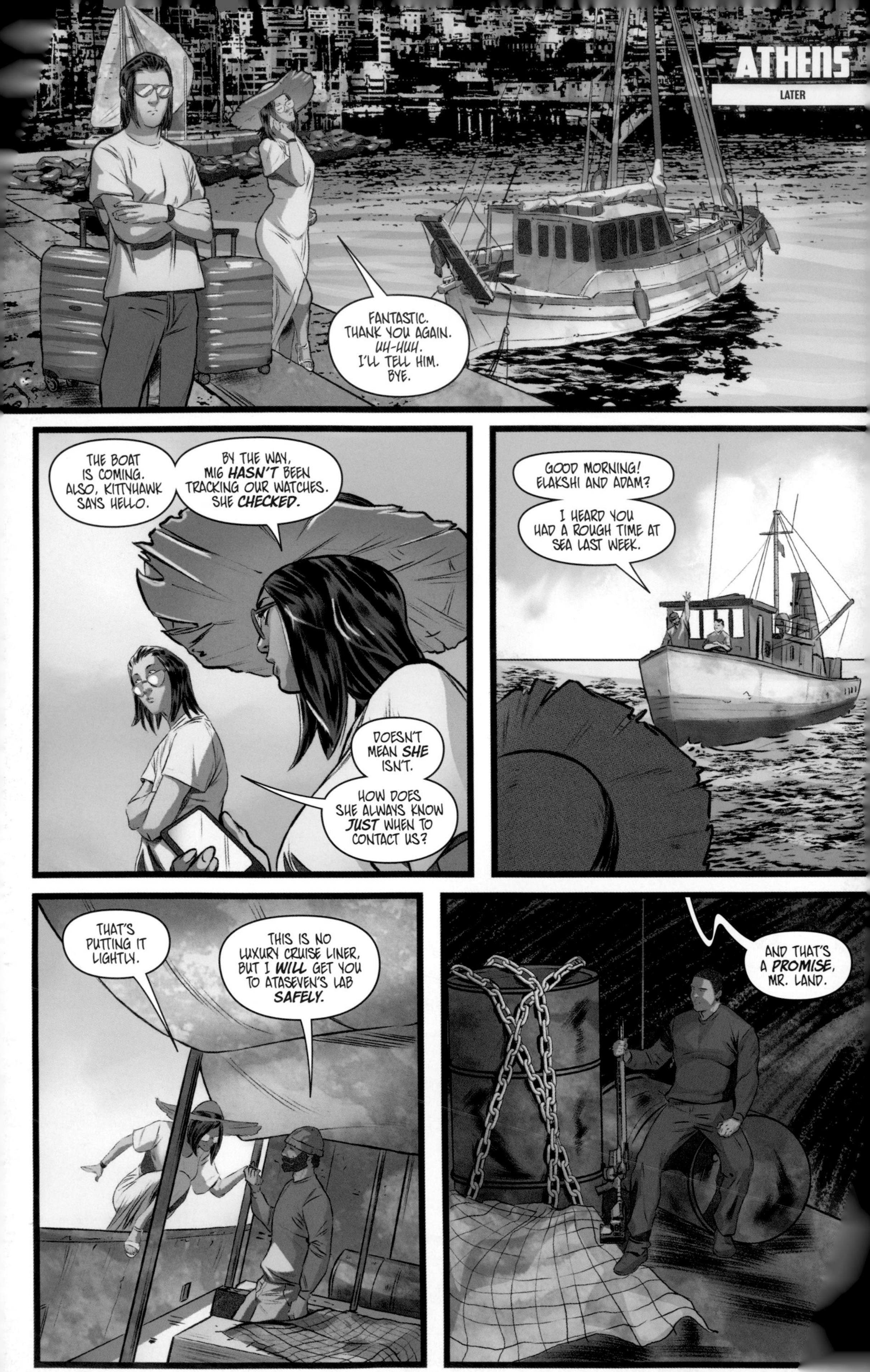
ATHENS
LATER
FANTASTIC. THANK YOU AGAIN. UH-HUH. I'LL TELL HIM. BYE.
THE BOAT IS COMING. ALSO, KITTYHAWK SAYS HELLO.
BY THE WAY, MI6 HASN'T BEEN TRACKING OUR WATCHES. SHE CHECKED.
DOESN'T MEAN SHE ISN'T.
HOW DOES SHE ALWAYS KNOW JUST WHEN TO CONTACT US?
GOOD MORNING! ELAKSHI AND ADAM?
I HEARD YOU HAD A ROUGH TIME AT SEA LAST WEEK.
THAT'S PUTTING IT LIGHTLY.
THIS IS NO LUXURY CRUISE LINER, BUT I WILL GET YOU TO ATASEVEN'S LAB SAFELY.
AND THAT'S A PROMISE, MR. LAND.

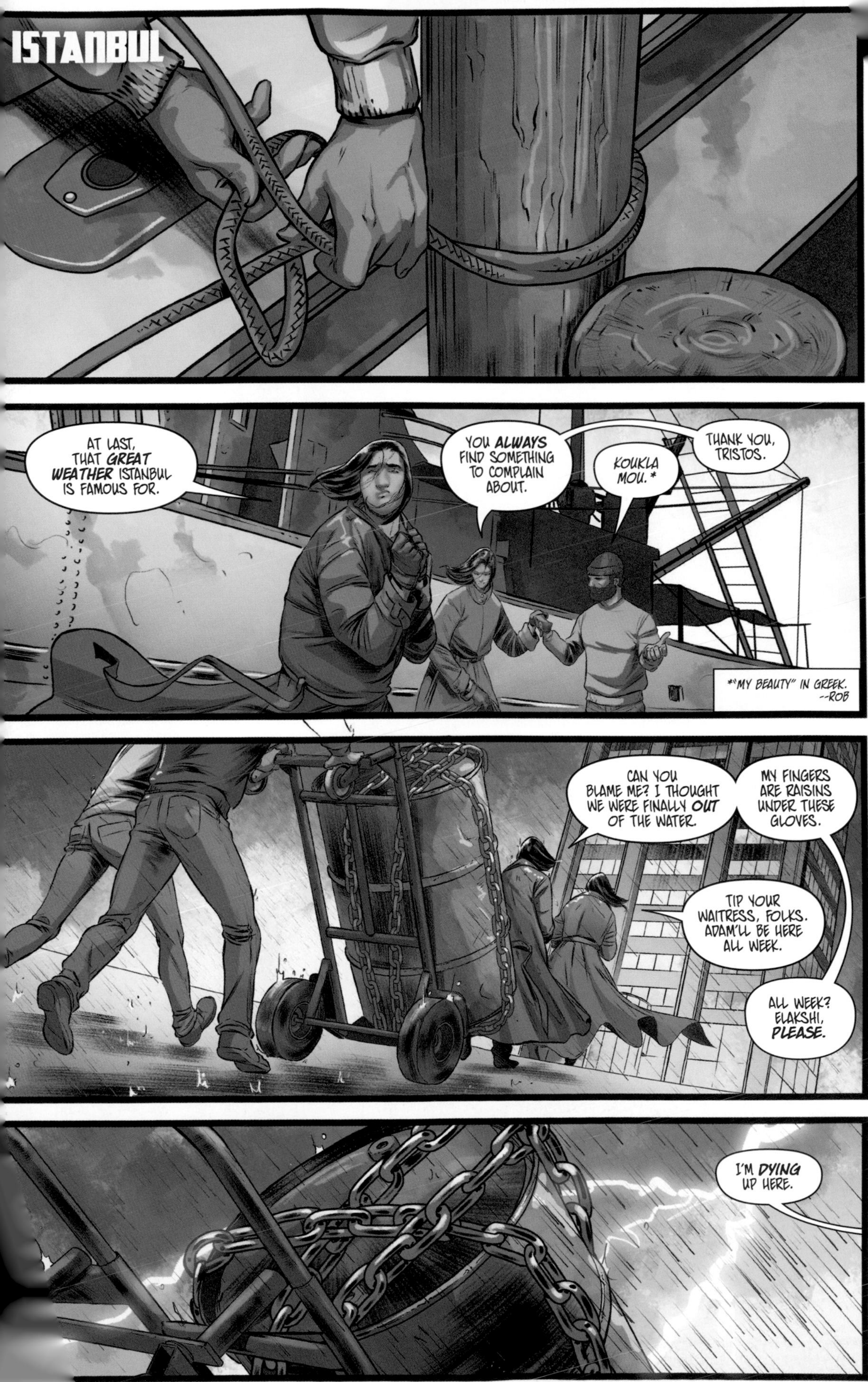
ISTANBUL
AT LAST, THAT GREAT WEATHER ISTANBUL IS FAMOUS FOR.
YOU ALWAYS FIND SOMETHING TO COMPLAIN ABOUT.
KOUKLA MOU.*
THANK YOU, TRISTOS.
*"MY BEAUTY" IN GREEK. --ROB
CAN YOU BLAME ME? I THOUGHT WE WERE FINALLY OUT OF THE WATER.
MY FINGERS ARE RAISINS UNDER THESE GLOVES.
TIP YOUR WAITRESS, FOLKS. ADAM'LL BE HERE ALL WEEK.
ALL WEEK? ELAKSHI, PLEASE.
I'M DYING UP HERE.

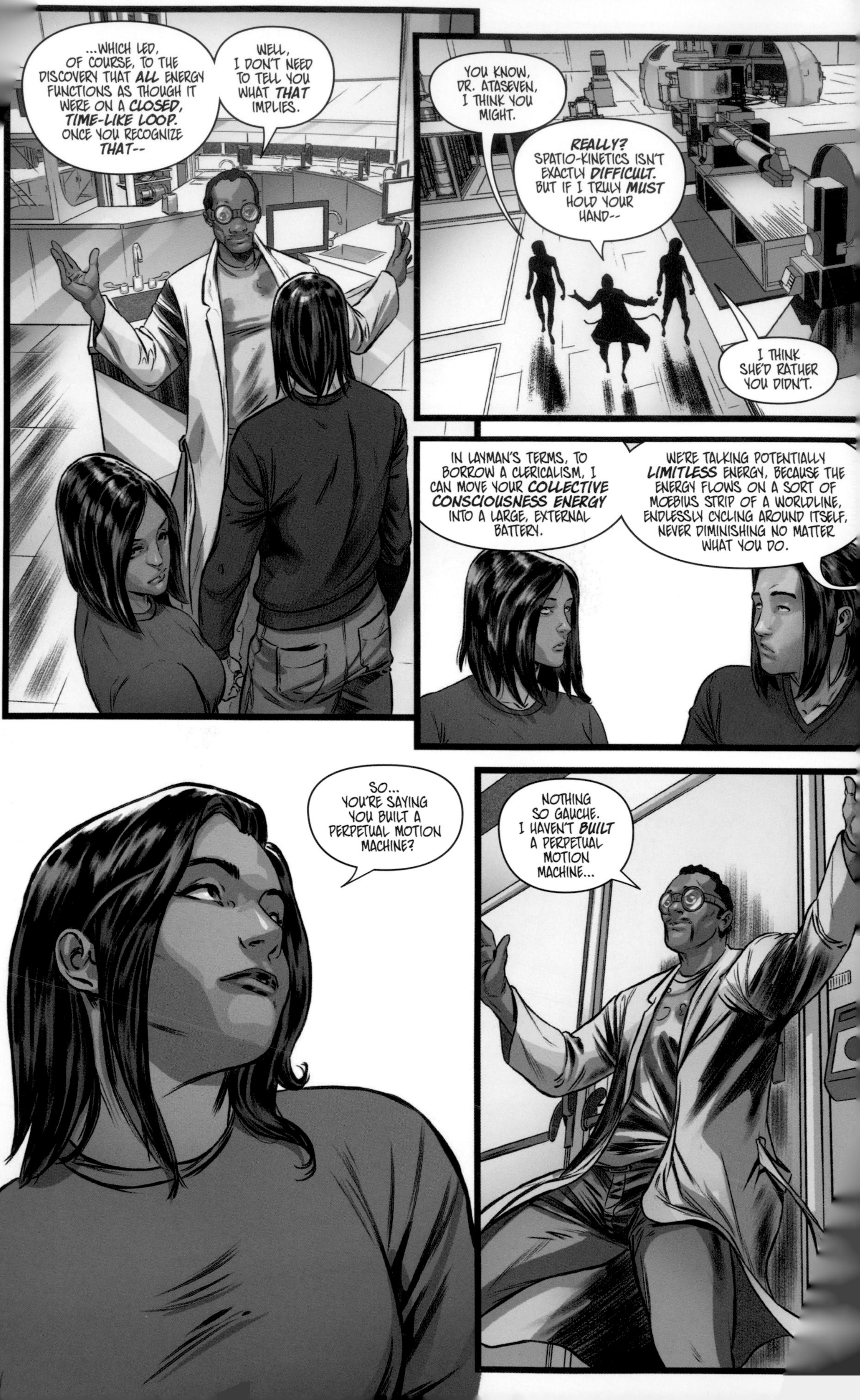
...WHICH LED, OF COURSE, TO THE DISCOVERY THAT ALL ENERGY FUNCTIONS AS THOUGH IT WERE ON A CLOSED, TIME-LIKE LOOP. ONCE YOU RECOGNIZE THAT--
WELL, I DON'T NEED TO TELL YOU WHAT THAT IMPLIES.
YOU KNOW, DR. ATASEVEN, I THINK YOU MIGHT.
REALLY? SPATIO-KINETICS ISN'T EXACTLY DIFFICULT. BUT IF I TRULY MUST HOLD YOUR HAND--
I THINK SHE'D RATHER YOU DIDN'T.
IN LAYMAN'S TERMS, TO BORROW A CLERICALISM, I CAN MOVE YOUR COLLECTIVE CONSCIOUSNESS ENERGY INTO A LARGE, EXTERNAL BATTERY.
WE'RE TALKING POTENTIALLY LIMITLESS ENERGY, BECAUSE THE ENERGY FLOWS ON A SORT OF MOEBIUS STRIP OF A WORLDLINE, ENDLESSLY CYCLING AROUND ITSELF, NEVER DIMINISHING NO MATTER WHAT YOU DO.
SO... YOU'RE SAYING YOU BUILT A PERPETUAL MOTION MACHINE?
NOTHING SO GAUCHE. I HAVEN'T BUILT A PERPETUAL MOTION MACHINE...

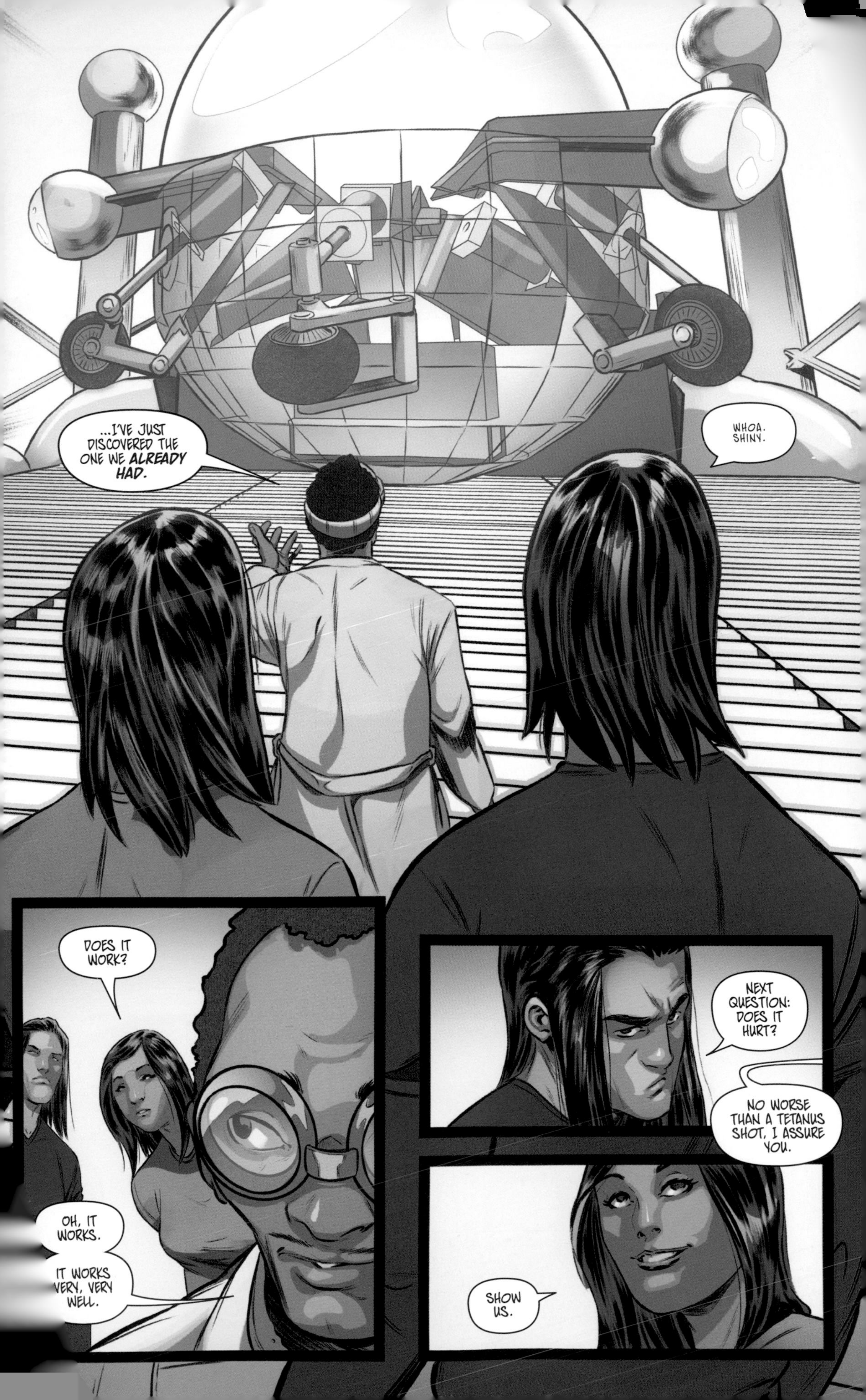
...I'VE JUST DISCOVERED THE ONE WE ALREADY HAD.
WHOA. SHINY.
DOES IT WORK?
OH, IT WORKS.
IT WORKS VERY, VERY WELL.
NEXT QUESTION: DOES IT HURT?
NO WORSE THAN A TETANUS SHOT, I ASSURE YOU.
SHOW US.

--OW RECORDING. MY NAME IS DR. *UZAY ATASEVEN*, AND THIS IS THE FIRST HUMAN TRIAL OF THE *TRANSFER SCAFFOLD*.

FAZEKA UPOR HAS VOLUNTEERED TO BE THE GUINEA PIG.

SAY HI, UPOR.

HI, UPOR.

HILARIOUS. DO YOU UNDERSTAND THE RISKS OF THIS PROCEDURE, UPOR?

ZAP ME, DOC. I'M TIRED OF BEING A HUMAN BATTERING RAM.

ACTIVATING SCAFFOLD IN FIVE... FOUR...

...THREE... TWO...

HNNNNNG!

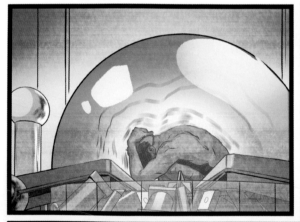

GIVE IT TO ME STRAIGHT, DOC.

WAS IT LYME DISEASE?

COOL, RIGHT?

WHO'S FIRST?

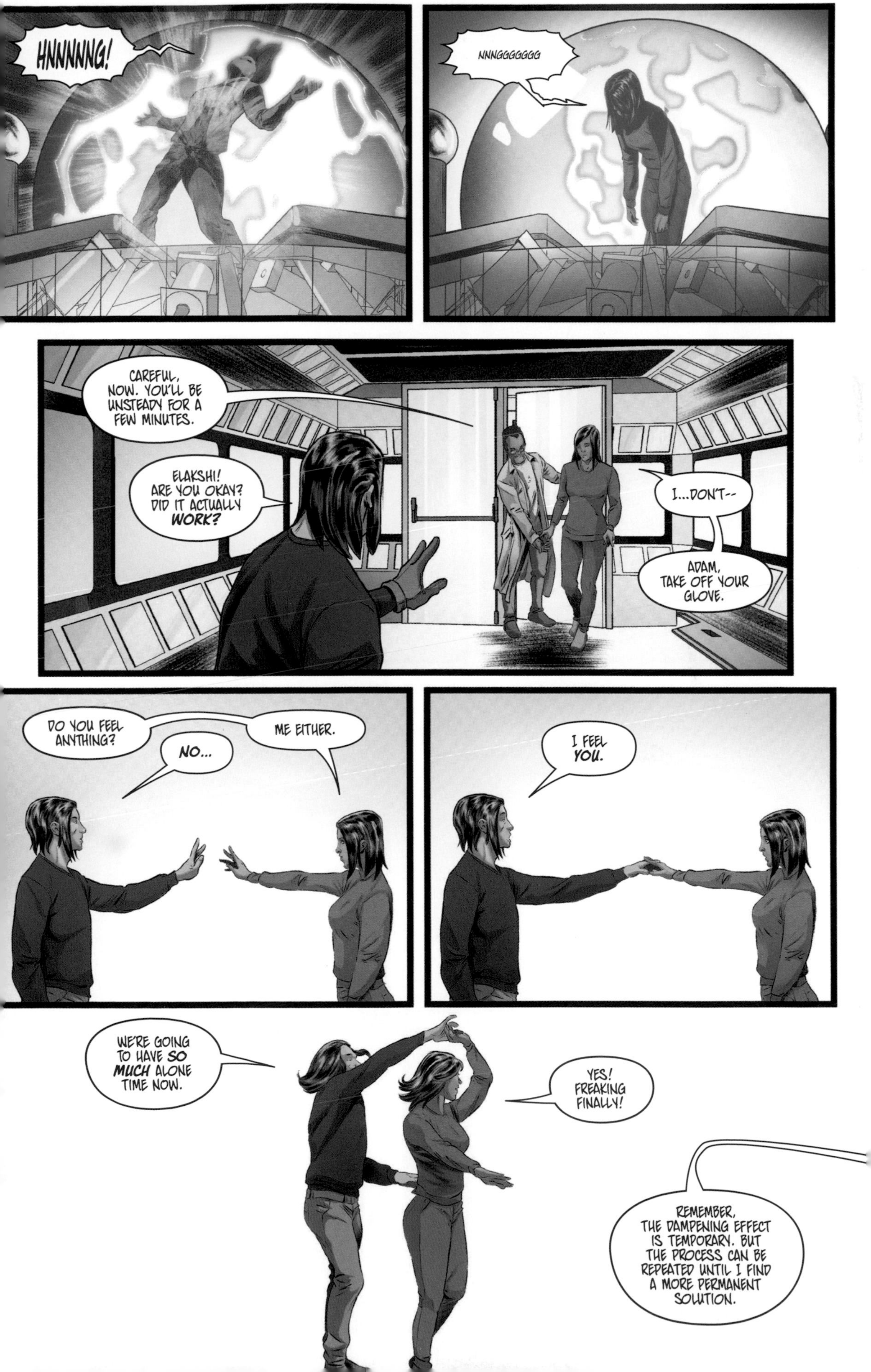
HNNNNG!
NNNGGGGGGG
CAREFUL, NOW. YOU'LL BE UNSTEADY FOR A FEW MINUTES.
ELAKSHI! ARE YOU OKAY? DID IT ACTUALLY WORK?
I...DON'T--
ADAM, TAKE OFF YOUR GLOVE.
DO YOU FEEL ANYTHING?
NO...
ME EITHER.
I FEEL YOU.
WE'RE GOING TO HAVE SO MUCH ALONE TIME NOW.
YES! FREAKING FINALLY!
REMEMBER, THE DAMPENING EFFECT IS TEMPORARY. BUT THE PROCESS CAN BE REPEATED UNTIL I FIND A MORE PERMANENT SOLUTION.

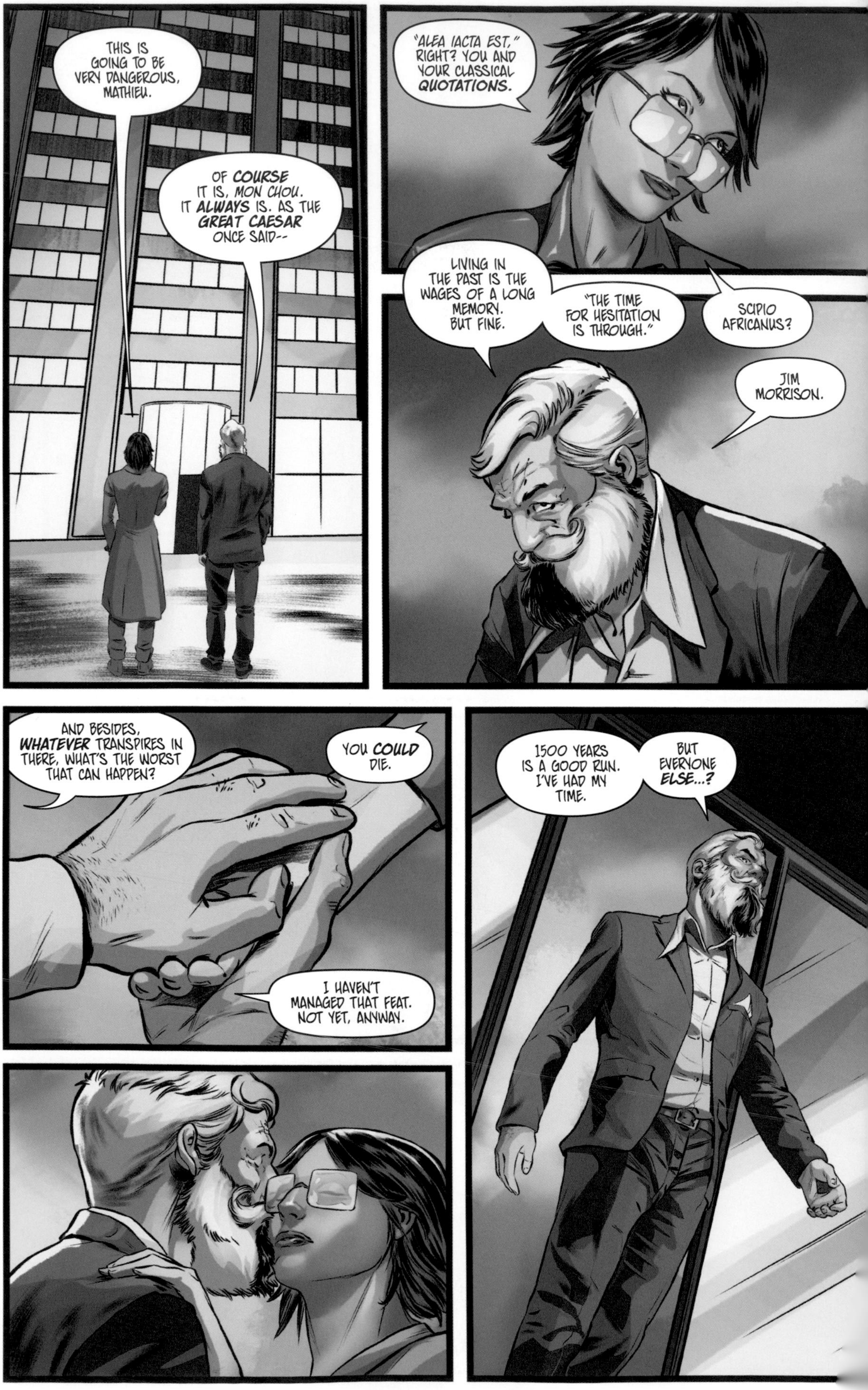
THIS IS GOING TO BE VERY DANGEROUS, MATHIEU.
OF **COURSE** IT IS, MON CHOU. IT **ALWAYS** IS. AS THE **GREAT CAESAR** ONCE SAID--
"ALEA IACTA EST," RIGHT? YOU AND YOUR CLASSICAL **QUOTATIONS**.
LIVING IN THE PAST IS THE WAGES OF A LONG MEMORY. BUT FINE.
"THE TIME FOR HESITATION IS THROUGH."
SCIPIO AFRICANUS?
JIM MORRISON.
AND BESIDES, **WHATEVER** TRANSPIRES IN THERE, WHAT'S THE WORST THAT CAN HAPPEN?
YOU **COULD** DIE.
I HAVEN'T MANAGED THAT FEAT. NOT YET, ANYWAY.
1500 YEARS IS A GOOD RUN. I'VE HAD MY TIME.
BUT EVERYONE **ELSE...?**

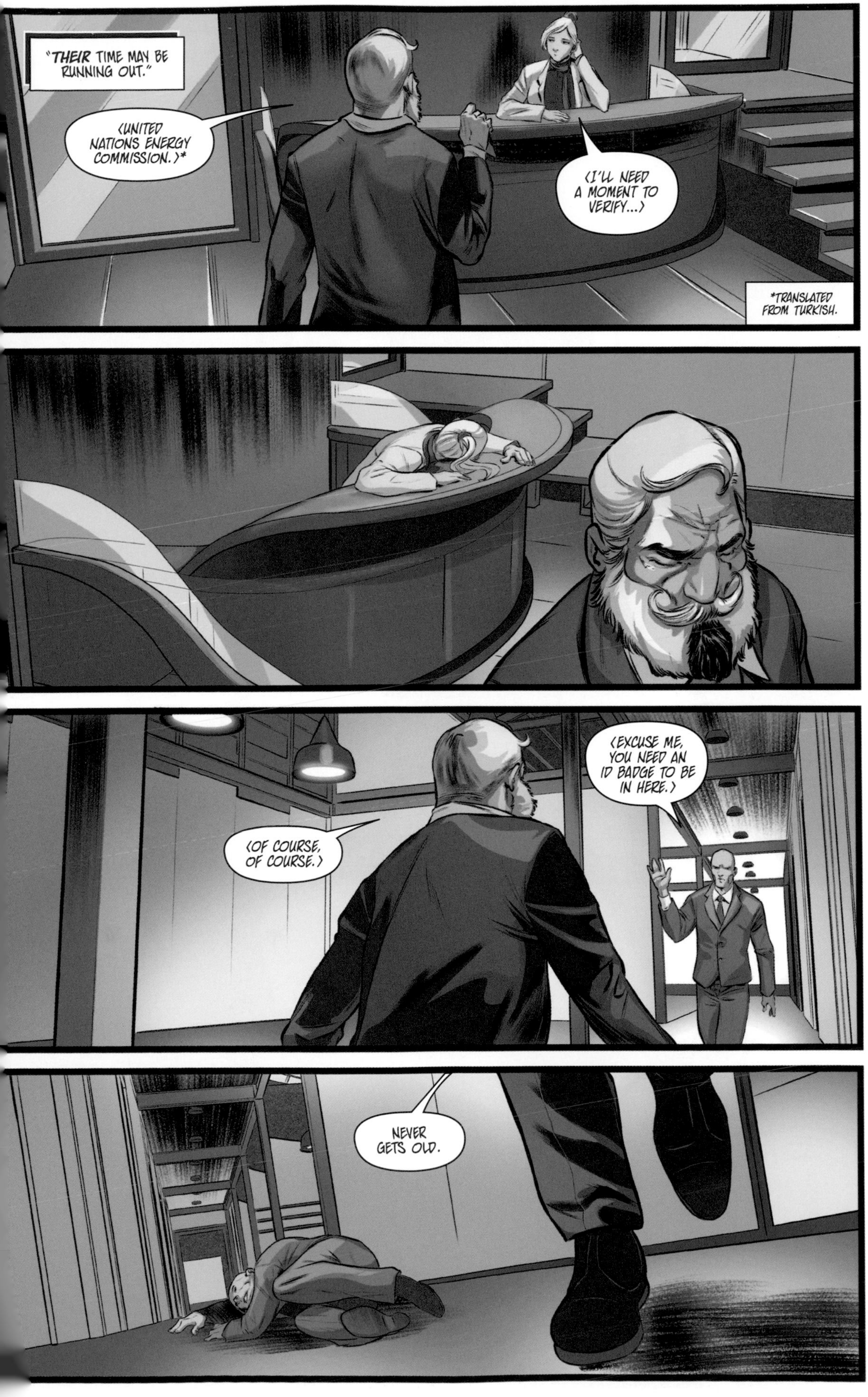
"THEIR TIME MAY BE RUNNING OUT."
‹UNITED NATIONS ENERGY COMMISSION.›*
‹I'LL NEED A MOMENT TO VERIFY...›
*TRANSLATED FROM TURKISH.
‹EXCUSE ME, YOU NEED AN ID BADGE TO BE IN HERE.›
‹OF COURSE, OF COURSE.›
NEVER GETS OLD.

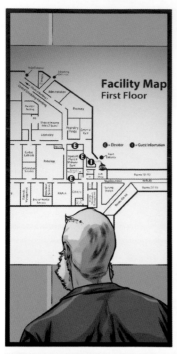

Facility Map
First Floor

SIMPLE ENOUGH.

HMM.

KA-KLINK

EXCUSE ME, MADEMOISELLE...

GAH!

WE NEED TO *TALK.*

WHAT NOW?

TELL ME, ELAKSHI LAND...

WHAT DO YOU REALLY KNOW ABOUT THE WOMAN YOU CALL *KITTYHAWK?*

I KNEW IT.

I GODDAMN **KNEW** IT.

KITTYHAWK'S BEEN PLAYING US FROM THE **START.**

YOU DON'T HAVE TO RUB IT IN.

NEITHER OF YOU CAN BE BLAMED. YOU WERE DESPERATE.

KITTYHAWK MADE SURE OF THAT.

I DON'T GET IT. WHY DID SHE TELL THAT MIG GUY HOW TO FIND US...

...WHILE ENSURING THAT WE ALWAYS ESCAPED?

TO KEEP US ON A LEASH. TO SCARE US. TO DISTRACT US.

TO MAKE US **DEPEND** ON HER.

RIGHT.

SO WHY SHOULD WE BELIEVE **YOU,** MYSTERIOUS STRANGER?

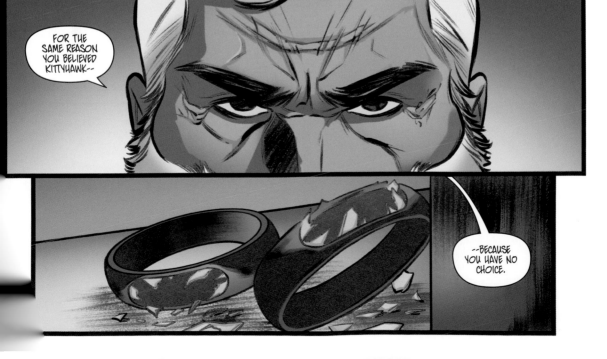

FOR THE SAME REASON YOU BELIEVED KITTYHAWK--

--BECAUSE YOU HAVE NO CHOICE.

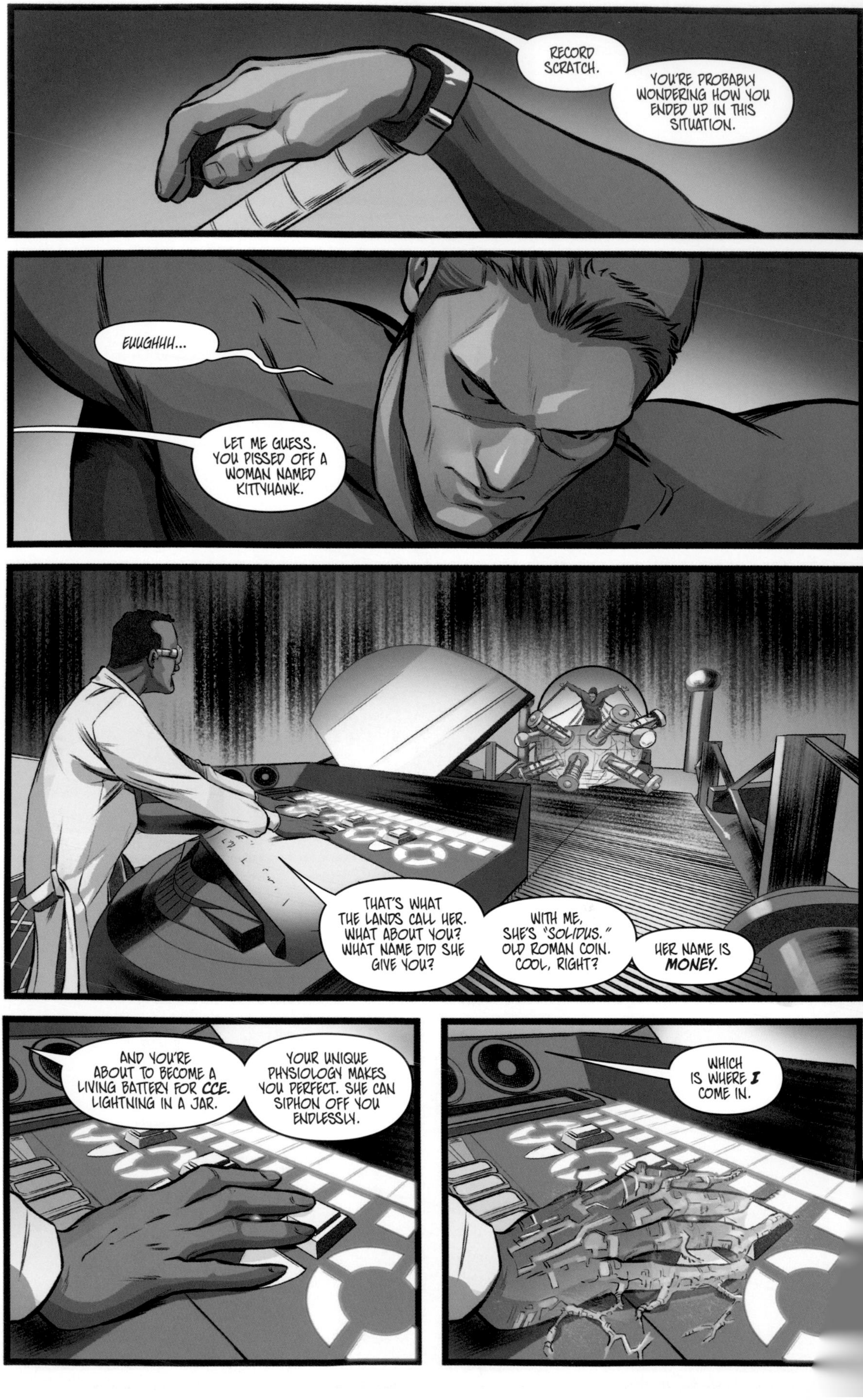
RECORD SCRATCH.
YOU'RE PROBABLY WONDERING HOW YOU ENDED UP IN THIS SITUATION.
EUUGHHH...
LET ME GUESS. YOU PISSED OFF A WOMAN NAMED KITTYHAWK.
THAT'S WHAT THE LANDS CALL HER. WHAT ABOUT YOU? WHAT NAME DID SHE GIVE YOU?
WITH ME, SHE'S "SOLIDUS." OLD ROMAN COIN. COOL, RIGHT?
HER NAME IS MONEY.
AND YOU'RE ABOUT TO BECOME A LIVING BATTERY FOR CCE. LIGHTNING IN A JAR.
YOUR UNIQUE PHYSIOLOGY MAKES YOU PERFECT. SHE CAN SIPHON OFF YOU ENDLESSLY.
WHICH IS WHERE I COME IN.

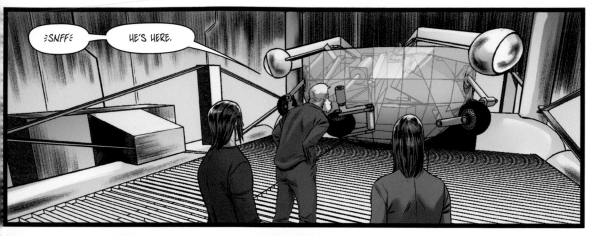
≈SNFF≈

HE'S HERE.

UH, WHERE? IS HE INVISIBLE?

REALLY, ADAM?

THAT WAS A SERIOUS QUESTION. THESE ARE STRANGE TIMES.

FSSSH

THAT SHOULD TAKE CARE OF THE SEAL. ELAKSHI? HAS YOUR POWER REBOUNDED?

NO, MERELY HIDDEN. OBSERVE.

≈UNF≈

THAT'S A YES.

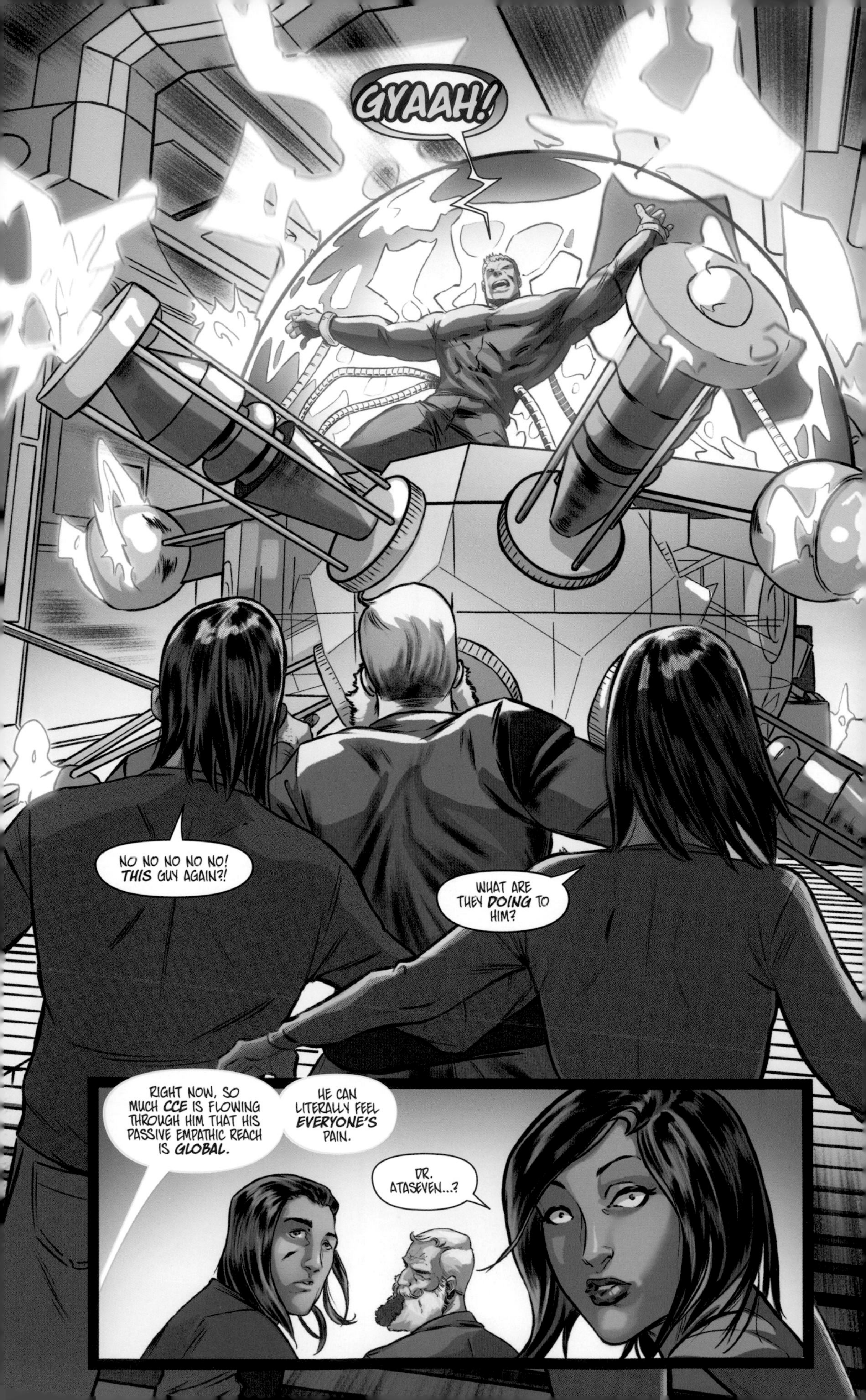
GYAAH!
NO NO NO NO NO! THIS GUY AGAIN?!
WHAT ARE THEY DOING TO HIM?
RIGHT NOW, SO MUCH CCE IS FLOWING THROUGH HIM THAT HIS PASSIVE EMPATHIC REACH IS GLOBAL.
HE CAN LITERALLY FEEL EVERYONE'S PAIN.
DR. ATASEVEN...?

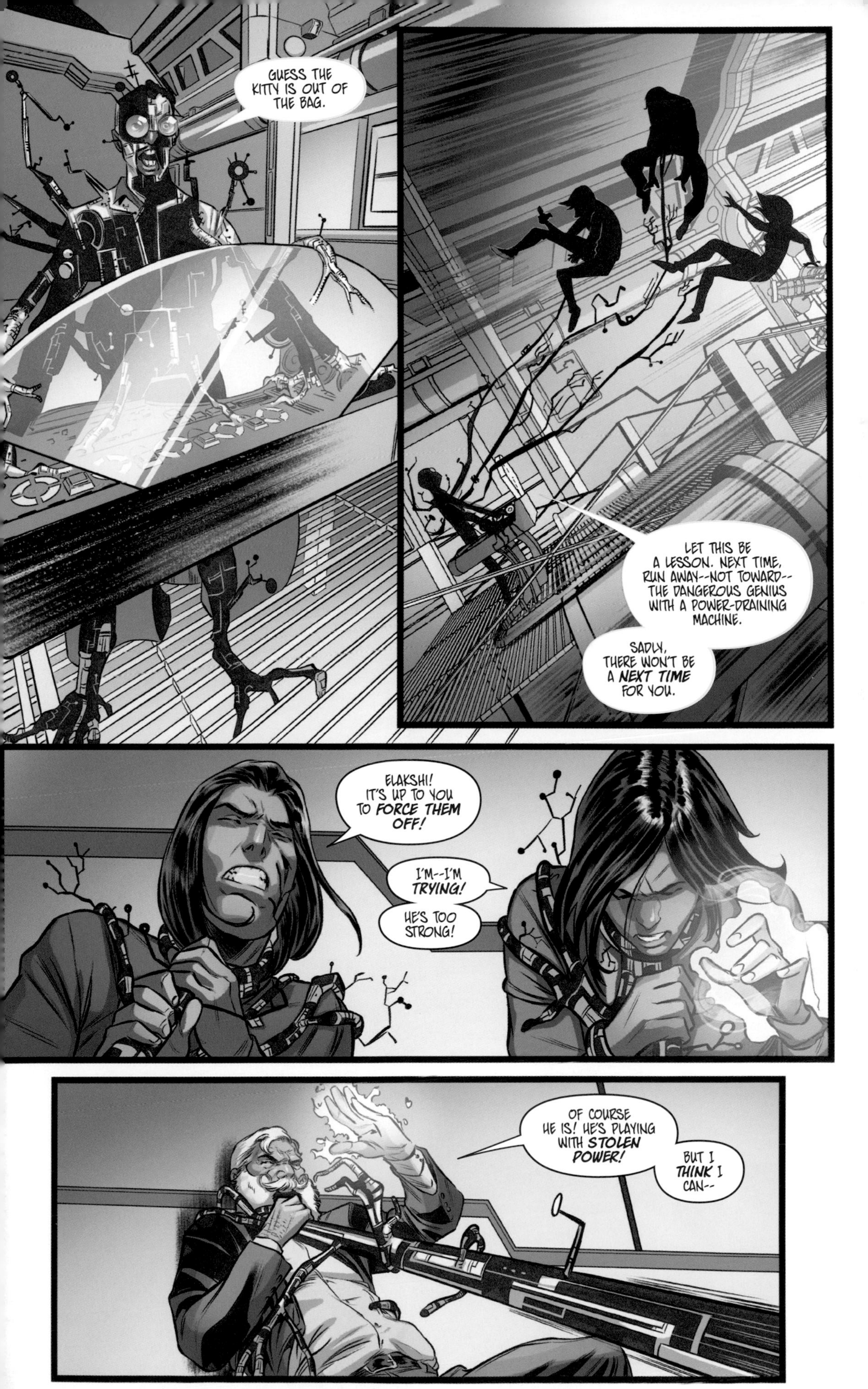
GUESS THE KITTY IS OUT OF THE BAG.
LET THIS BE A LESSON. NEXT TIME, RUN AWAY--NOT TOWARD--THE DANGEROUS GENIUS WITH A POWER-DRAINING MACHINE.
SADLY, THERE WON'T BE A NEXT TIME FOR YOU.
ELAKSHI! IT'S UP TO YOU TO FORCE THEM OFF!
I'M--I'M TRYING!
HE'S TOO STRONG!
OF COURSE HE IS! HE'S PLAYING WITH STOLEN POWER!
BUT I THINK I CAN--

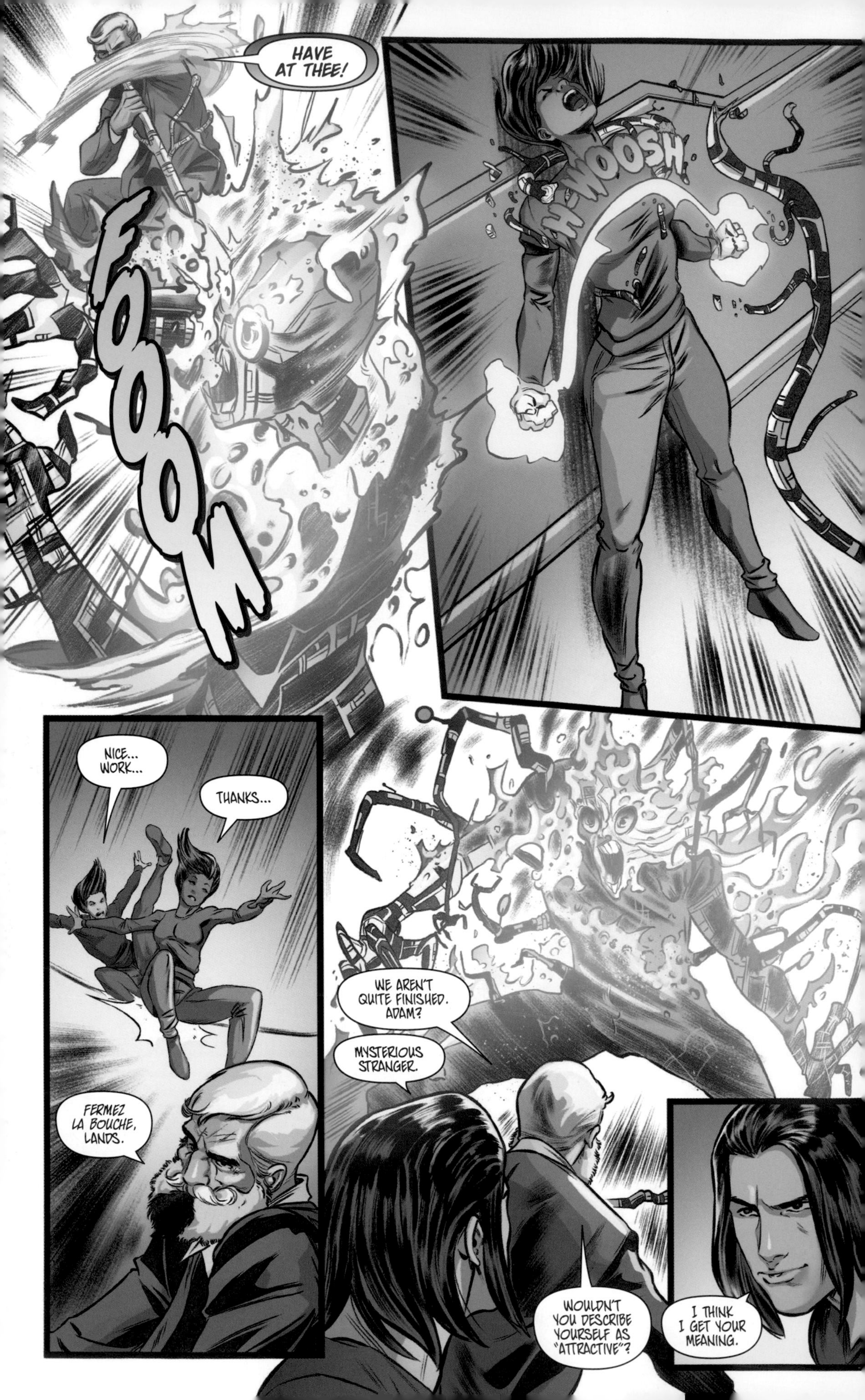
HAVE AT THEE!
FOOOOM
WOOSH
NICE... WORK...
THANKS...
FERMEZ LA BOUCHE, LANDS.
WE AREN'T QUITE FINISHED. ADAM?
MYSTERIOUS STRANGER.
WOULDN'T YOU DESCRIBE YOURSELF AS "ATTRACTIVE"?
I THINK I GET YOUR MEANING.

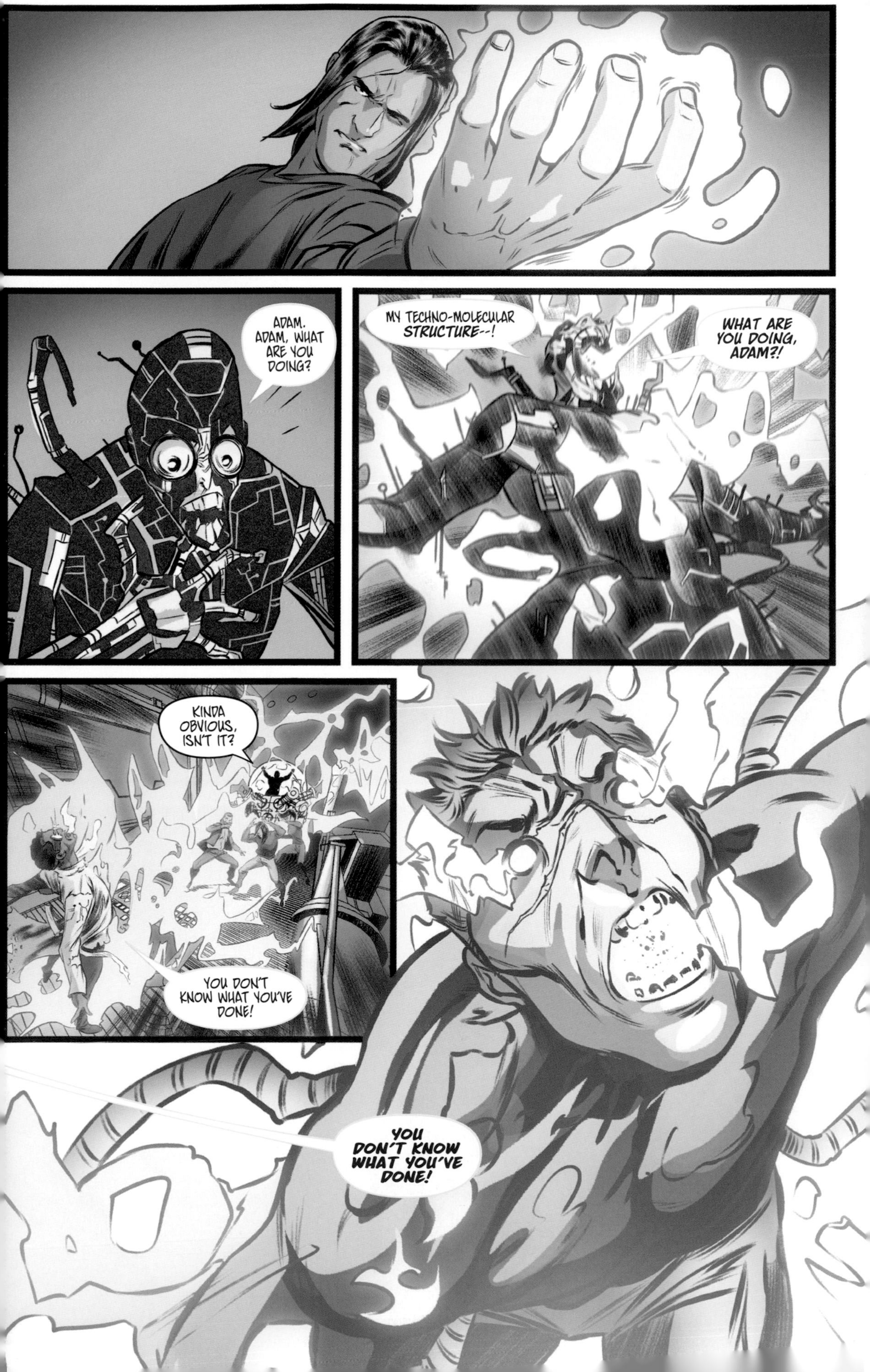
ADAM. ADAM, WHAT ARE YOU DOING?
MY TECHNO-MOLECULAR STRUCTURE--!
WHAT ARE YOU DOING, ADAM?!
KINDA OBVIOUS, ISN'T IT?
YOU DON'T KNOW WHAT YOU'VE DONE!
YOU DON'T KNOW WHAT YOU'VE DONE!

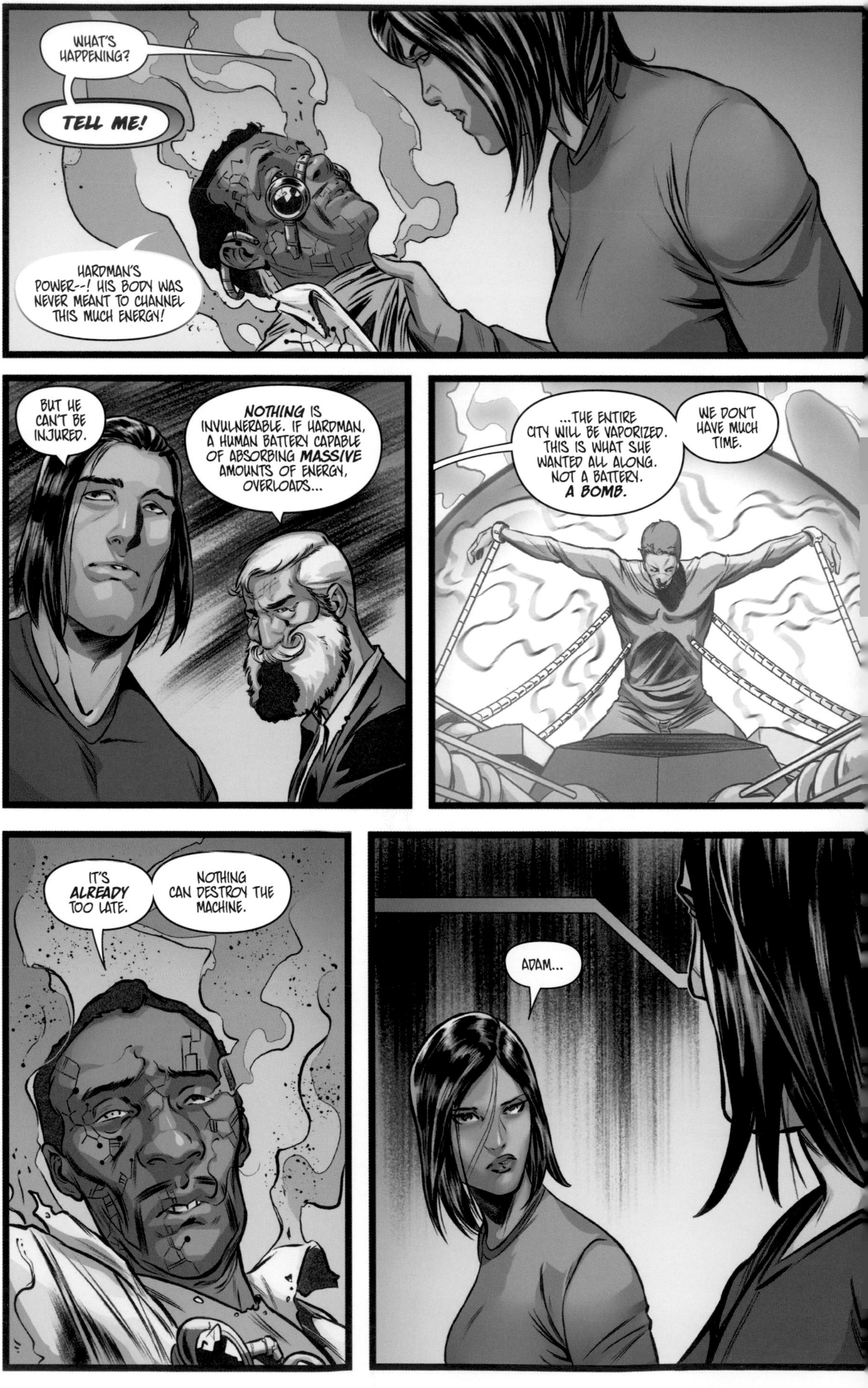
WHAT'S HAPPENING?
TELL ME!
HARDMAN'S POWER--! HIS BODY WAS NEVER MEANT TO CHANNEL THIS MUCH ENERGY!
BUT HE CAN'T BE INJURED.
NOTHING IS INVULNERABLE. IF HARDMAN, A HUMAN BATTERY CAPABLE OF ABSORBING MASSIVE AMOUNTS OF ENERGY, OVERLOADS...
...THE ENTIRE CITY WILL BE VAPORIZED. THIS IS WHAT SHE WANTED ALL ALONG. NOT A BATTERY. A BOMB.
WE DON'T HAVE MUCH TIME.
IT'S ALREADY TOO LATE.
NOTHING CAN DESTROY THE MACHINE.
ADAM...

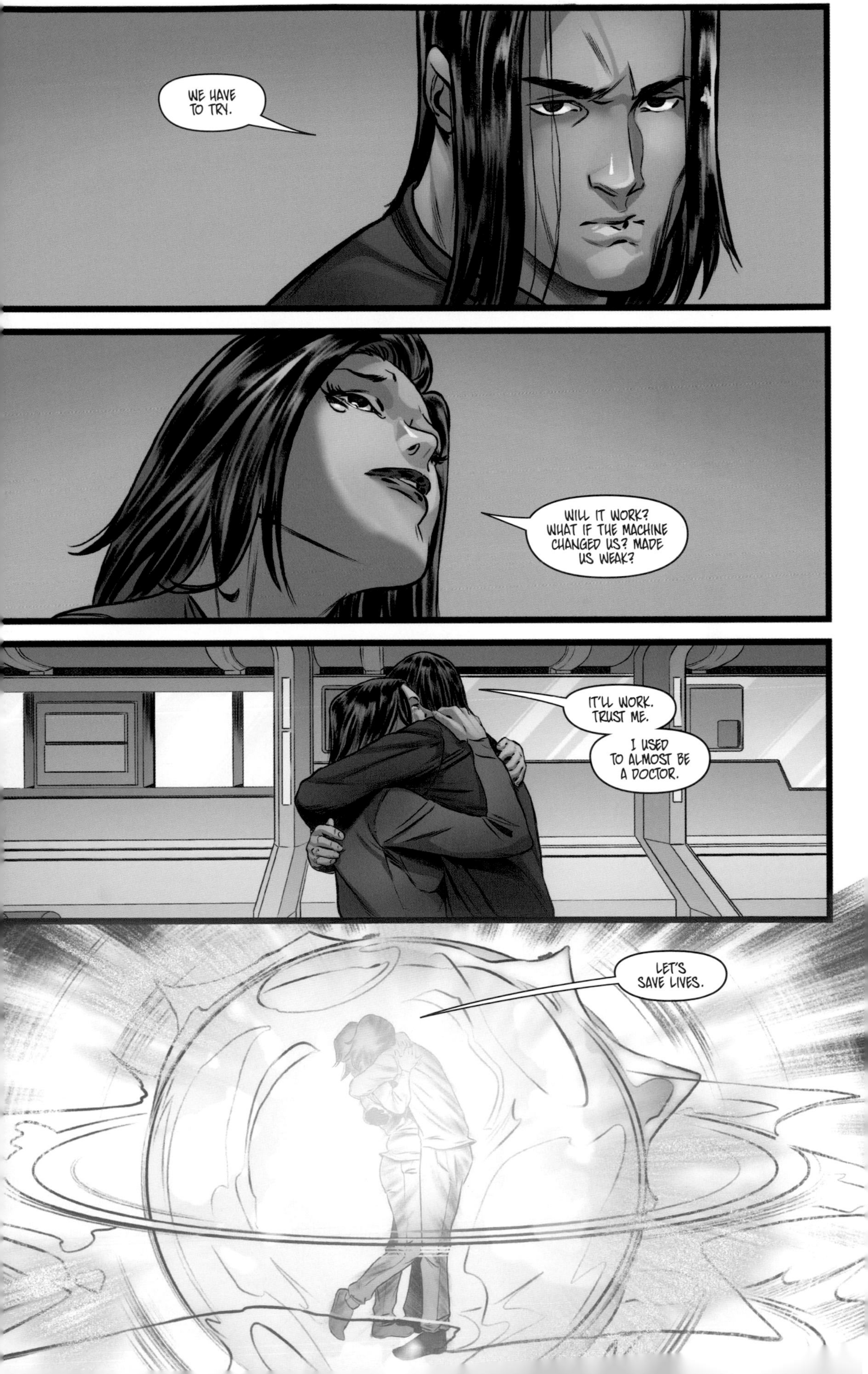
WE HAVE TO TRY.
WILL IT WORK? WHAT IF THE MACHINE CHANGED US? MADE US WEAK?
IT'LL WORK. TRUST ME.
I USED TO ALMOST BE A DOCTOR.
LET'S SAVE LIVES.

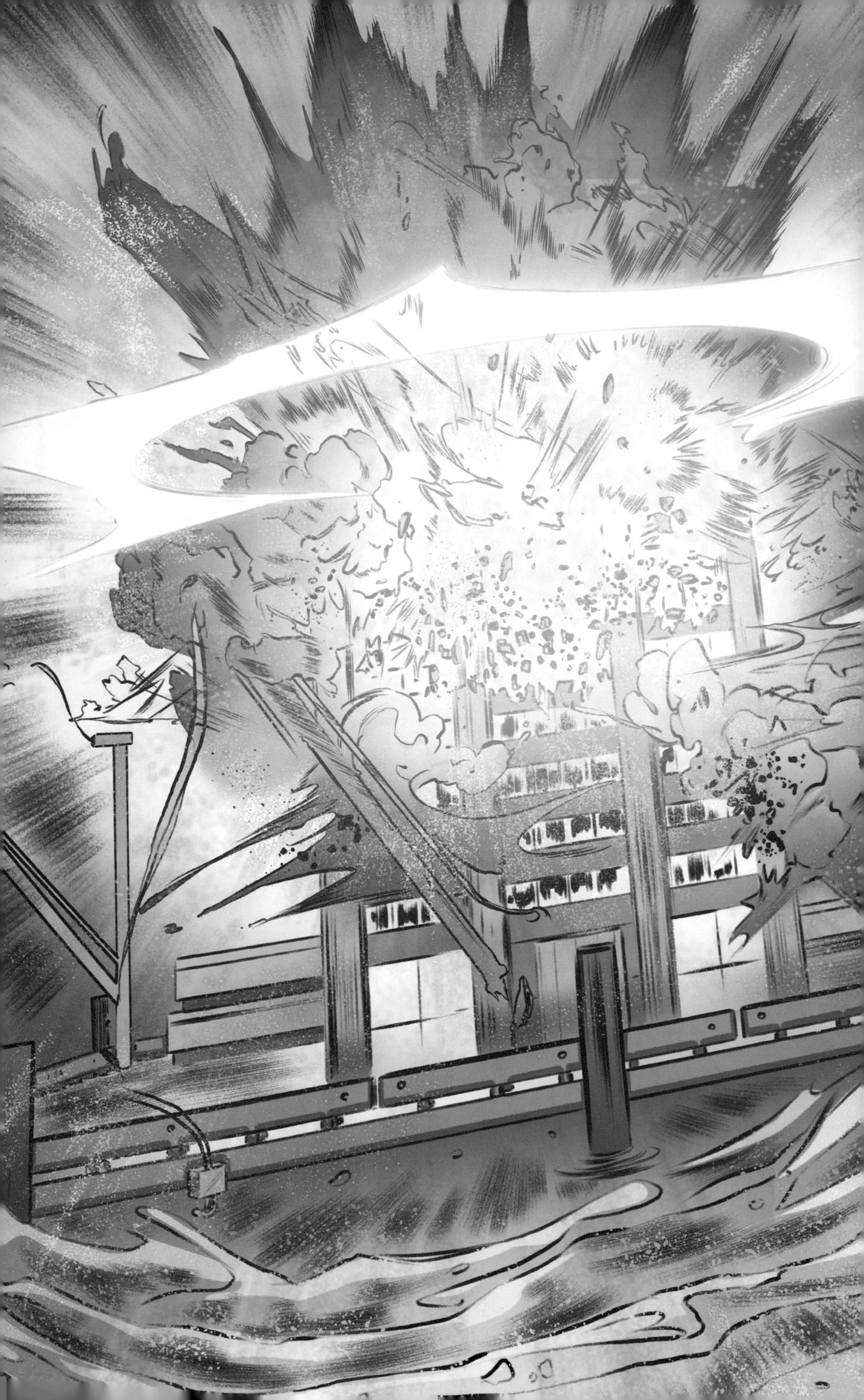

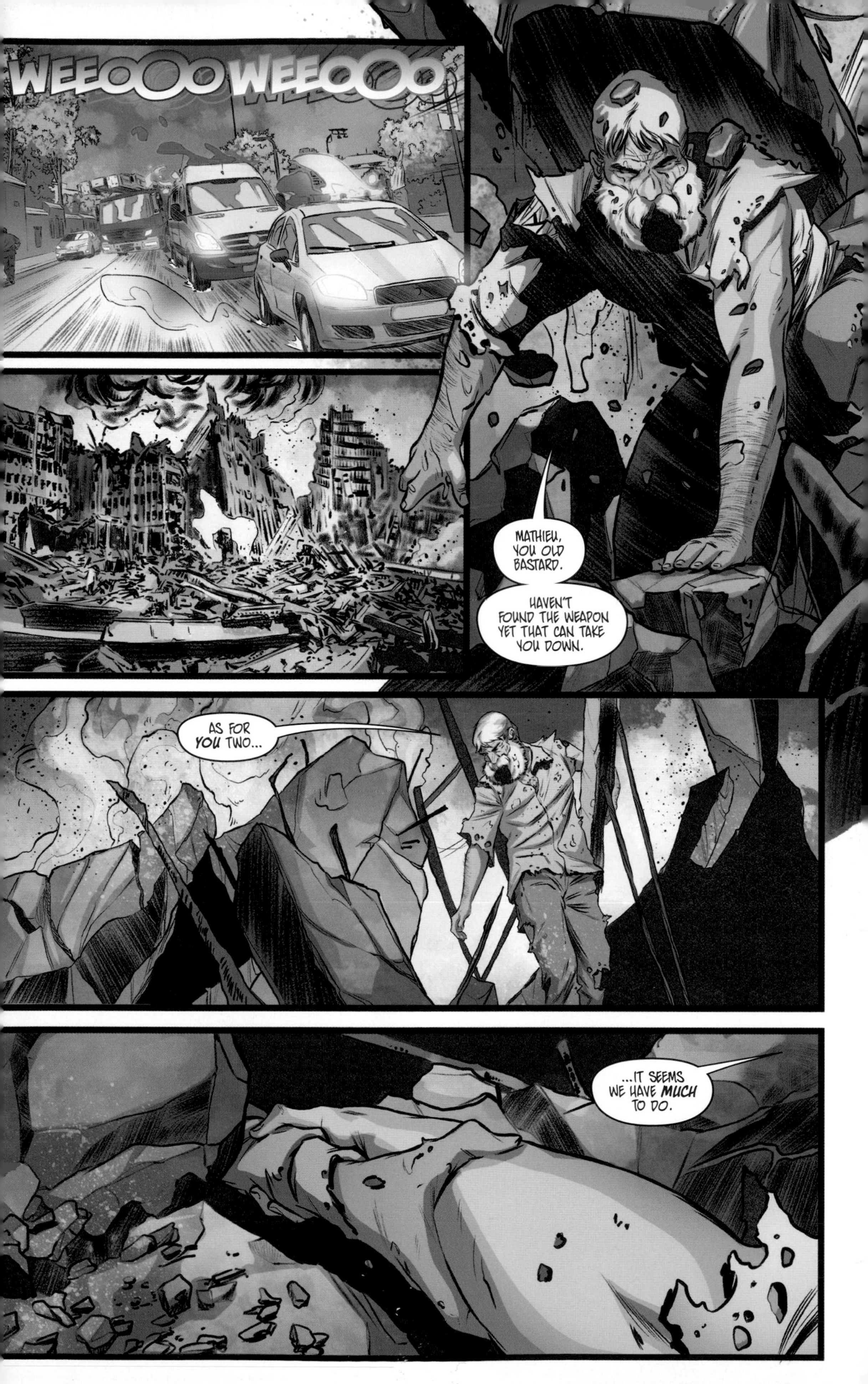
WEEOOO WEEOOO
MATHIEU, YOU OLD BASTARD.
HAVEN'T FOUND THE WEAPON YET THAT CAN TAKE YOU DOWN.
AS FOR YOU TWO...
...IT SEEMS WE HAVE MUCH TO DO.

MEANWHILE

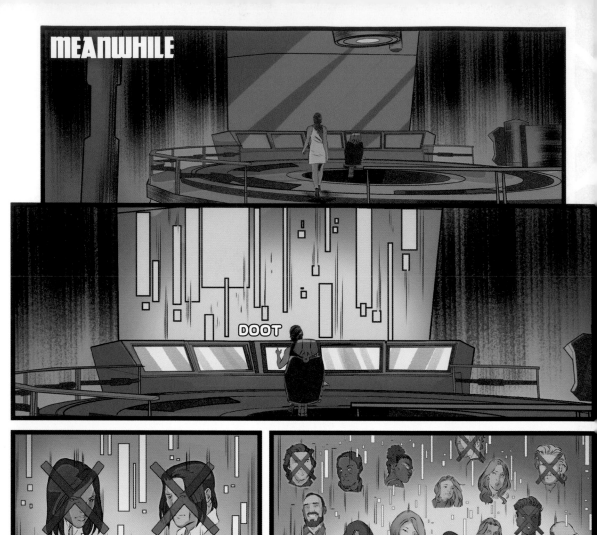

DOOT

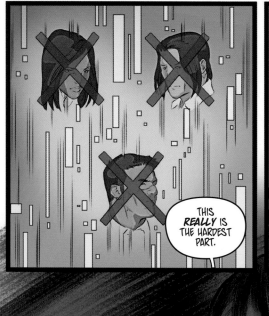

THIS *REALLY* IS THE HARDEST PART.

BUT THAT WAS JUST ONE ANGLE. THERE ARE ALWAYS OTHERS.

AND SOON, THE WHOLE *WORLD* WILL KNOW MY NAME.

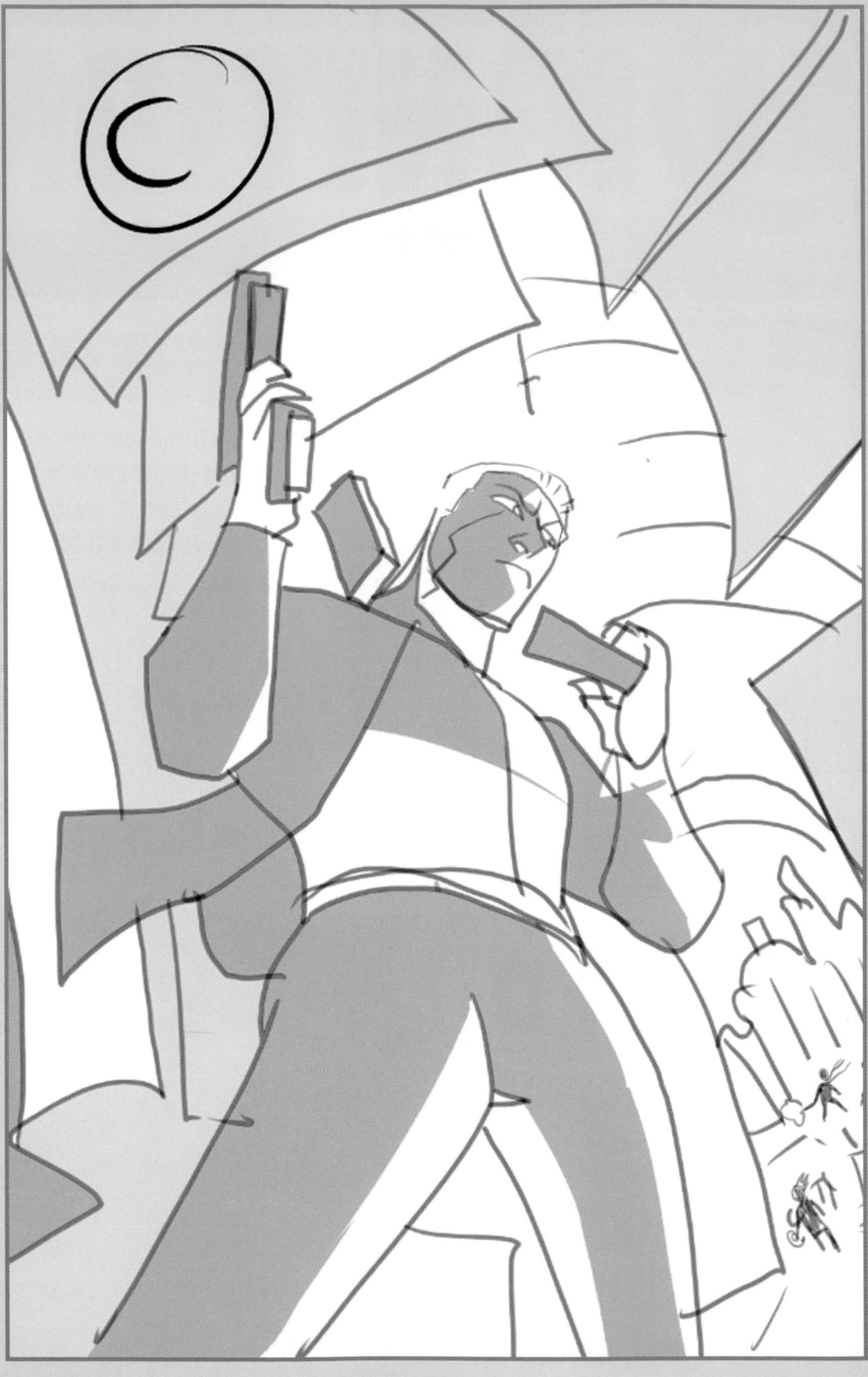

Original sketch for the **Strangelands #6** cover by Michael Avon Oeming.

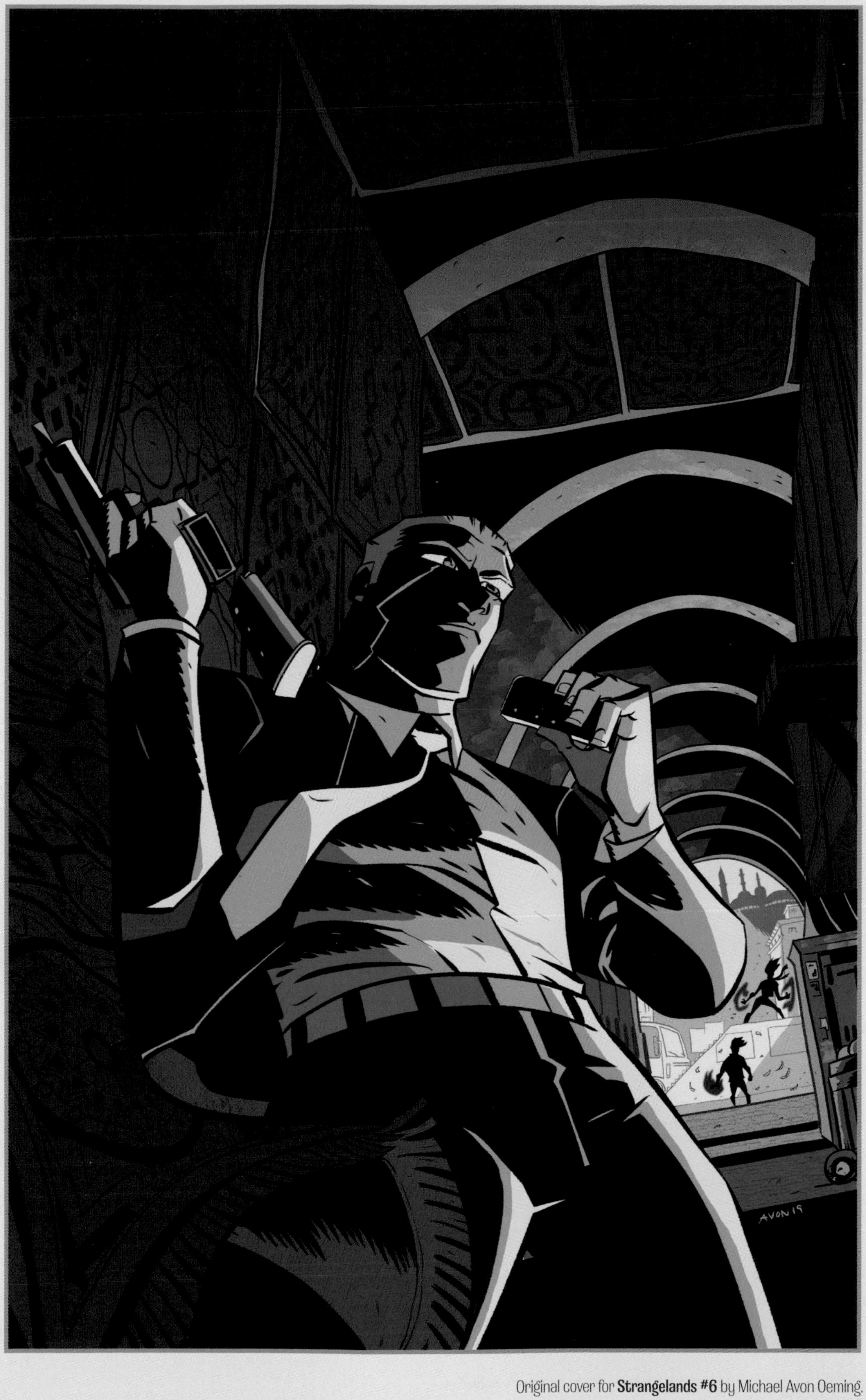
AVON 19

Original cover for **Strangelands #6** by Michael Avon Oeming.

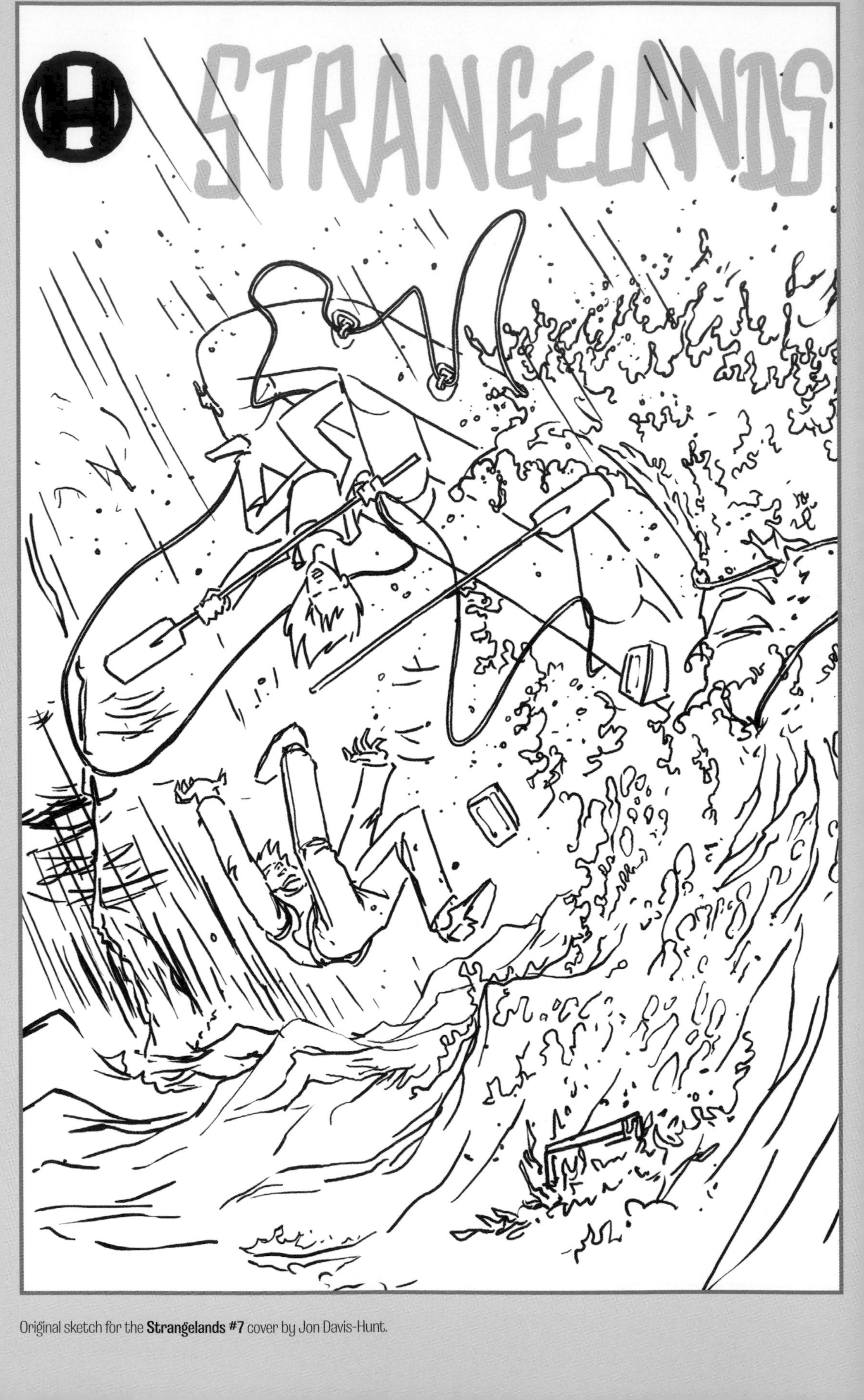
STRANGELANDS

Original sketch for the **Strangelands #7** cover by Jon Davis-Hunt.

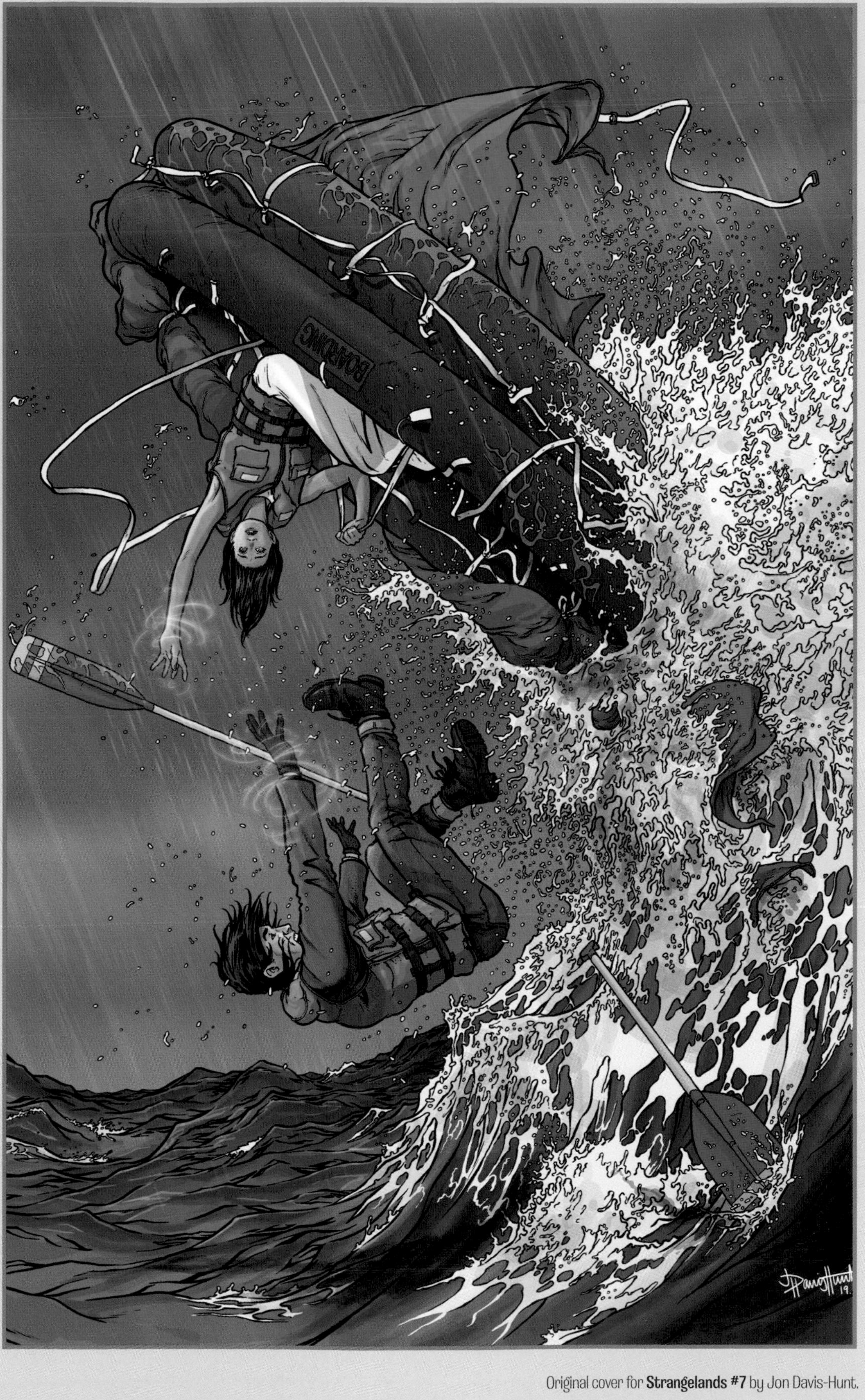
BOARDING

Original cover for **Strangelands #7** by Jon Davis-Hunt.

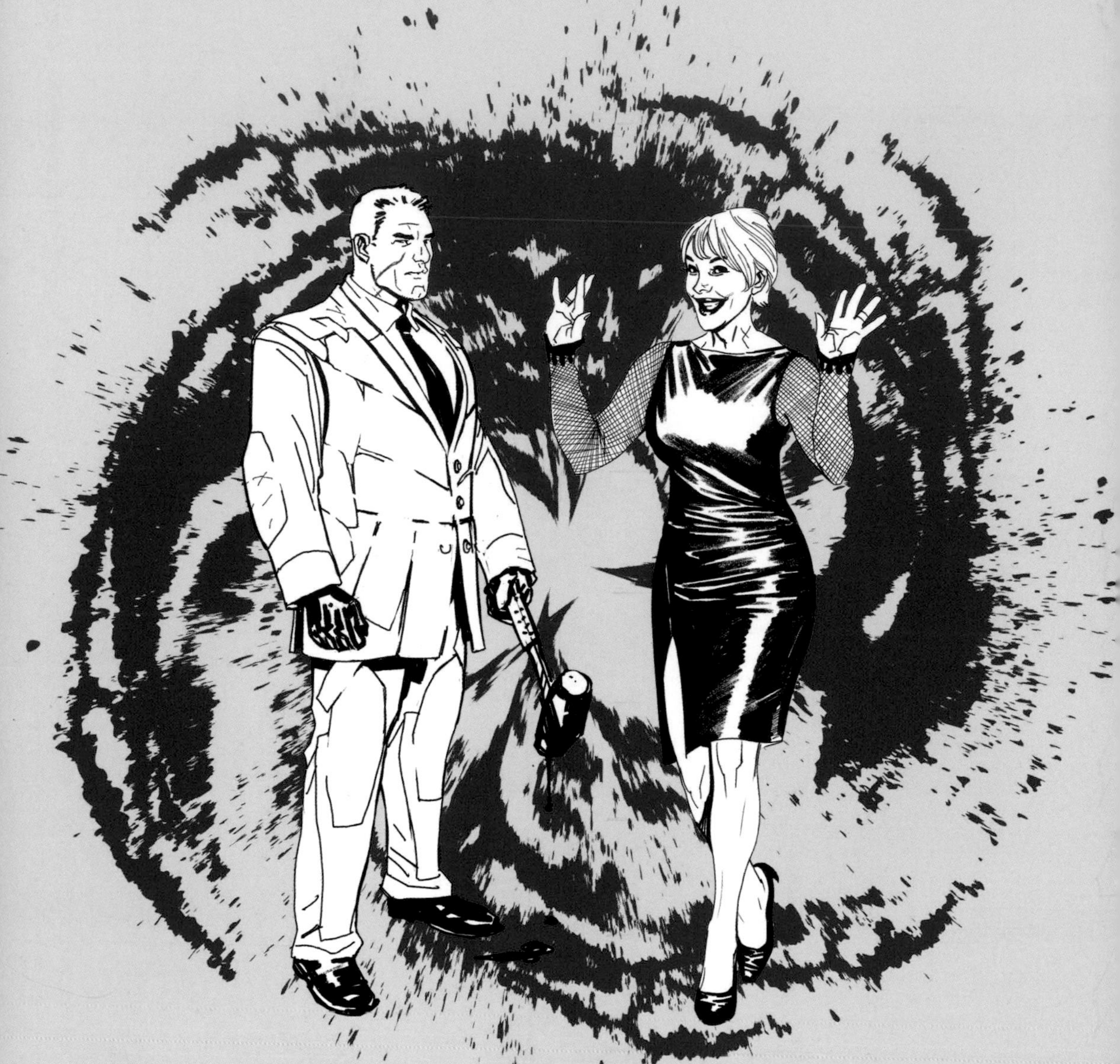

Original **Strangelands** character designs for Agent Hardman (left) and master manipulator "Kittyhawk" (right) by H1 Architect Yanick Paquette.